The Thinker's Library, No. 83.

RELIGION WITHOUT REVELATION

By

JULIAN HUXLEY, M.A., D.Sc., F.R.S.

LONDON:

WATTS & CO.,

5 & 6 JOHNSON'S COURT, FLEET STREET, E.C.4

First published in the Thinker's Library, 1941
Second Impression, 1945

" How is religion still possible? " This question is posed by so able a thinker as Dr. Merz as the question of paramount importance, and he can find only a paradoxical answer.

It is a question which seems to be taken seriously by many otherwise intelligent persons, who are thereby stranded in the end on all sorts of hidden sandbanks. They do not ask : How is walking still possible? They do not ask : How is hunger still possible? Yet it is really the same kind of question.

It is always marvellous to find how people worry themselves over unnecessary problems, and spin the most fantastic webs of abstruse speculation around even the simplest things. Religion, if it is anything at all, must be a natural organic function, like walking, like eating, better still, like loving. For the closest analogy and, indeed, real relationship of religion, is with the function of reproduction and the emotions of sex. The functions of eating and walking are more or less necessary to life in their rhythmic recurrences, and it is legitimate in their absence to endeavour to stimulate them into action. But the function of religion, like that of love, is not necessary to life, nor may it with any certainty be stimulated into activity. Need it? These functions are either working within you or they are not. If not, then it is clear that your organism is in no need of them at the present moment, and perhaps is born without the aptitude to experience them. And if so, there are those who will tell you that you represent a superior type of humanity. Therefore, whether if not so, or whether so, why worry?

I do not indeed myself think that the inaptitude for the function of religion—ancient as the religious emotions are—represents a higher stage of development. But I am sure that either the function is there or it is not there, and that no intellectual speculations will take its place or hasten its manifestations.

Religion, like love, develops and harmonizes our rarest and most extravagant emotions. It exalts us above the commonplace routine of our daily life, and it makes us supreme over the world. But, like love also, it is a little ridiculous to those who are unable to experience it. And since they can survive quite well without experiencing it, let them be thankful, as we also are thankful.—HAVELOCK ELLIS (in *The Forum*, 1924).

Printed and Published in Great Britain by C. A. Watts & Co. Limited,
5 & 6 Johnson's Court, Fleet Street, London, E.C.4

PREFACE

I AM very much pleased that the Rationalist Press Association are including an abridged version of my *Religion without Revelation* in their excellent (and remarkably cheap) series, The Thinker's Library.

The book was written thirteen years ago, and in the interval I have changed some of my views, as all thinking men are likely to do on any vast and general subject. But I have not changed my views on what I suppose is the central thesis of the book. I can perhaps sum this up as follows :—

First, religion is an important higher function of man. Secondly, the form which religion takes will and must vary with changes in human life and human outlook. Thirdly, there is usually a serious time-lag in adjusting that form to new conditions as they arise. And, finally, the time is ripe—over-ripe—for a radical change in the form of the official religions of the Western World.

A large part of the book is accordingly devoted to a retranslation of the realities at the base of orthodox Christianity into modern terms. Such a retranslation must deal with the intellectual formulations of theology, with the ritual expressions of religious feeling, and with the central spiritual attitudes at religion's core.

As regards theology, there are a number of people

who are now saying that religion and science are no longer at loggerheads with each other. This I altogether deny. The dispute is not so noisy nor so obvious as in the days when literal or semi-literal acceptance of the Bible was a pre-requisite for orthodoxy, and when therefore picturesque controversies, dealing with the Gadarene swine or the precise age of the world or man's alleged descent from monkeys, could catch the limelight. But it is still fundamental, for it concerns not merely the nature but the existence of God. True, there are many divines who have so diluted the idea of God with philosophical milk-and-water that God now can, very conveniently, mean something totally different to the theologian and to the ordinary man in the street : true also that there are a number of scientists who have come to the conclusion that some sort of God exists somewhere in the background. But even if God, in the sense of an external and somehow personal or at least spiritual Power behind phenomena, has lost much of His earlier authority, and is in fact tending to fade away, like the Cheshire Cat in *Alice*, until only a faint cosmic smile remains, yet this question of God or no God, external Power or no external Power, non-human absolute values as against human evolving values—this question is fundamental. Until it is settled, and the idea of God relegated to the past with the idea of ritual magic and other products of primitive and unscientific human thought, we shall never get the new religion we need. In that new religion, man must make up his mind to take upon himself his full burden, by acknowledging that he is the highest entity of which he has any knowledge, that his values are the only basis for any categorical imperative, and that he must work out both his own salvation and destiny, and the standards on which they are based. To put off this burden on to the shoulders of an imaginary God is to shrink from full responsibility, and to hinder man from arriving at his full stature.

Nor is it true to-day that theology is irrelevant to spiritual and moral attitude. What I have just written is proof to the contrary. It is obvious that any religion which lays primary emphasis on salvation in the next world will be something of an obstacle towards getting the best out of this world as speedily as possible. It is equally obvious that any religion which stresses the need for propitiating an external Power will be diverted away from the more essential task of using and organising the spiritual forces that lie within each individual. " The Kingdom of Heaven is within you " is a saying that has not been sufficiently taken into account in orthodox theology.

Once we have rid ourselves of this doctrine of a Divine Power external to ourselves, we can get busy with the real task of dealing with our inner forces. These are largely subconscious or latent : any developed religion must find ways of helping the individual to face his subconscious, and to realize the latent possibilities of his spirit. And obviously it must enable him to detach his feelings and beliefs to a certain considerable extent from concrete objects and to build them up into an organized whole in a given relation with his view of the universe rather than attached to particular objects of desire. Only through such an inner reservoir of spirit can maturity attain to a serene and satisfying existence. Much has already been done, especially by oriental religions, to work out the empirical basis of attaining to inner states of serenity, non-attachment, and ecstasy, but it remains both to put this knowledge on a scientific footing, and, still more important, to relate the attainment of such states to the less contemplative ideals of the Western World, and to its more scientific outlook.

Meanwhile we are confronted with the spectacle of social movements of a religious nature, such as Communism and Nazism, taking the place of traditional theological religion in large areas of the modern world. I regard this as a symptom and a portent of the rise of humanist religions to pre-eminence. It marks a crisis in world thought, just as did the passage from the primitive religions of animism, magic, mana, and tabu to religion on the theistic level. The parallel can be carried further. Just as many of the earlier manifestations of theistic religion were crude and horrible—such as beast-gods, human sacrifice, or extreme sacerdotalism—so these early manifestations of humanist and social religions are crude and horrible, with their erection of the State as a divine monster above the individual, their worship of power for its own sake, their deliberate creation of enemies to persecute, their equally deliberate suppression not only of freedom of thought, but of all activities not linked with the ends of the State.

It is urgent that we who are happy enough to live in free lands should think out the basis on which a socially-grounded humanist religion could develop healthily, into something of value to evolving life, instead of as a menace to it.

JULIAN HUXLEY.

London,
   December, 1940.

CONTENTS

CHAPTER I

A PRELIMINARY STATEMENT

Science . . . makes impossible any religion but the highest.—Canon B. H. STREETER, *Reality* (1927).

To mistake the world, or the nature of one's soul, is a dangerous error. He that thinks the Heavens and the Earth not his, can hardly use them. . . . Whatever we misapprehend we cannot use, nor well enjoy what we cannot use.—THOMAS TRAHERNE, *Centuries of Meditations*.

A system of dogmas may be the ark within which the Church floats safely down the flood-tide of history. But the Church will perish unless it opens its window and lets out the dove to search for an olive branch. Sometimes even it will do well to disembark on Mount Ararat and build a new altar to the divine Spirit—an altar neither in Mount Gerizim nor at Jerusalem.—A. N. WHITEHEAD, *Religion in the Making* (1927).

If we are to assume that anybody has designedly set this wonderful universe going, it is perfectly clear to me that he is no more entirely benevolent and just, in any intelligible sense of the words, than that he is malevolent and unjust.—T. H. HUXLEY, *Life and Letters*.

I am not so lost in lexicography as to forget that *words are the daughters of earth, and that things are the sons of heaven.*—SAMUEL JOHNSON, Preface to his *Dictionary*.

Vox dei revelatur in rebus.—FRANCIS BACON.

Truth can never be opposed to Truth.—Canon BUCKLAND, *Bridgewater Treatises*, vol. i. (1837).

> You say there is no substance here,
>   One great reality above :
> Back from that void I shrink in fear,
>   And child-like hide myself in love :
> Show me what angels feel. Till then
> I cling, a mere weak man, to men.
>   —WILLIAM CORY, *Mimnermus in Church*.

1

Every new mind is a classification. . . . But in all un-
balanced minds the classification is idolized, passes for the
end and not for a speedily exhaustible means, so that the
walls of their system blend to their eye in the remote horizon
within the walls of the universe. They cannot imagine how
you aliens have any right to see—how you can see !—R. W.
EMERSON, *Essays*.

The fact that a believer is happier than a sceptic is no
more to the point than the fact that a drunken man is happier
than a sober one. The happiness of credulity is a cheap and
dangerous quality.—G. BERNARD SHAW.

I HAVE called this book *Religion without Revelation* in
order to express at the outset my conviction that
religion of the highest and fullest character can co-
exist with a complete absence of belief in revelation
in any straightforward sense of the word, and in that
kernel of revealed religion, a personal God.

This will probably be a new conception to most
people. Accordingly I shall have to spend a good
deal of my limited space in justifying my case with
the aid of evidence and argument. I propose at the
start to state my beliefs briefly in their main outlines,
without the attempt at full justification by reasoned
argument. This will give my readers a preliminary
view. I shall then come to exposition and argument;
and, finally, having to the best of my ability dis-
posed of objections and adduced evidence in favour
of my own view, shall again, though in a different
form and with a more adequate background, present
what seem to me the right conclusions.

What then do I believe? I believe, in the first
instance, that it is necessary to believe something.
Complete scepticism does not work. On the other
hand, I believe equally strongly that it is always
undesirable and often harmful to believe without
proper evidence. Everything which we believe,
except the logical necessities of mathematics and
formal logic, is believed on external evidence of one
sort or another, although the evidence may have been
assimilated so long ago, or so completely, or so in-

tuitively, that we are not conscious of it. To take a simple and trivial example : when we say that a ball which we see in the distance is spherical, we are basing this statement on the frequently repeated evidence of our past experience, that objects which appear to the eye of a particular shape and with a particular kind of pattern of light and shade are, when explored by touch, found to possess a particular shape we call spherical; and we had to learn all this very thoroughly (although we have by now forgotten all about the learning process) when we were babies. But even when there is not this necessary interpretation of the evidence of one sense in terms of the experience derived from another, but a direct utilization of the materials provided by one sense only, we are still believing on evidence. When I feel a marble with my fingers, my eyes being blindfolded, I can judge directly by touch that it is a single spherical object. But everybody knows (or, if he does not, let him immediately try the very simple but fundamental experiment) that if I cross two adjacent fingers and feel the marble between their crossed tips, it will be obstinately judged to be double, in spite of all knowledge to the contrary.

Thus even the simple judgments of sense may be illusions, and when I say that I believe something because I saw or heard it, I am backing the view that I did not happen to be deluded. When we come to more complicated beliefs, such as a belief that so-and-so is really angry with us although he is doing his best to appear friendly, or that someone else is an honest man and will never take an unfair advantage, it is still more evident that we are all the time weighing evidence and arriving at a conclusion (however intuitively) on the balance. And we are often wrong. How frequently it turns out that A's apparent anger was only dyspepsia, or that we were sadly mistaken as to B's honesty !

Apart from intellectual mistakes or sensory delusions, however, a still more potent source of error is emotional distortion. It is a perfectly obvious fact, which even serious investigators have not always escaped, to have their conclusions coloured by their desires, to see what they want to see, and, even more, not to see what they would prefer to overlook. An angry man is a notoriously bad witness; and the judgments of first love about the beloved object are quite generally discounted, and that not only by cynics.

There is thus a certain practical difficulty. We must believe something, for otherwise we should never act. On the other hand, we must not believe everything, or believe too readily, or we shall act wrongly. Most people would say that they were completely justified in the certain belief that the sun will rise next morning; on the other hand, there is for this no inherent necessity of the same nature as the inherent necessity for two and two to make four; something might perfectly well happen to prevent it rising; and we might believe in the existence of this something.

Experience has quite definitely shown (if only humanity could be persuaded to profit by her !) that some reasons for holding a belief are much more likely to be justified by the event than others. It might be naturally supposed, for instance, that the best of all reasons for belief was a strong conviction of certainty accompanying the belief. Experience, however, shows that this is not so, and that, as a matter of fact, conviction by itself is more likely to mislead than it is to guarantee truth. On the other hand, lack of assurance and persistent hesitation to come to any belief whatever are an equally poor guarantee that the few beliefs which are arrived at are sound. Experience also shows that assertion, however long continued, although it is unfortunately with many people an effective enough means of inducing belief, is not in any way a ground for holding it.

Neither is a claim to be the recipient of a revelation the least guarantee that belief in the subject of the revelation is justified; for both madmen and false prophets have made the claim.

The method which has proved effective, as matter of actual fact, in providing a firm foundation for belief wherever it has been capable of application, is what is usually called the scientific method. I believe firmly that the scientific method, although slow and never claiming to lead to complete truth, is the only method which in the long run will give satisfactory foundations for beliefs. The scientific method is the method which, in the intellectual sphere, is the counterpart of that method recommended by the apostle in the moral sphere—test all things; hold fast to that which is good. It consists in demanding facts as the only basis for conclusions; and of consistently and continuously testing any conclusions which may have been reached, against the test of new facts and, wherever possible, by the crucial test of experiment. It consists also (and this is not sufficiently recognized by the generality of people) in full publication of the evidence on which conclusions are based, so that other workers may have the advantage of the facts, to assist them in new researches, or, as frequently occurs, to make it possible for them to put a quite different interpretation on the facts.

There are, however, all sorts of occasions on which the scientific method is not applicable. That method involves slow testing, frequent suspension of judgment, restricted conclusions. The exigencies of everyday life, on the other hand, often make it necessary to act on a hasty balancing of admittedly incomplete evidence, to take immediate action, and to draw conclusions in advance of the evidence. It is also true that such action will always be necessary, and necessary in respect of ever larger issues; and this in spite of the fact that one of the most important trends of civilization is to remove sphere after sphere of life out of the domain of such intuitive judgment into the domain of rigid calculation based on science. It is here that belief plays its most important rôle. When we cannot be certain, we must proceed in part by faith—faith not only in the validity of our own capacity of making judgments, but also in the existence of certain outer realities, pre-eminently moral and spiritual realities. It has been said that faith consists in acting always on the nobler hypothesis; and though this definition is a trifle rhetorical, it embodies a seed of real truth.

Finally, however (and this is a truth which has often been wholly unrecognized, and never popular), there are other occasions on which belief is not only not demanded, but is, in the phraseology of medicine, contra-indicated. When there exists no evidence or next to no evidence, and when the conclusion to which we should come to and can have no influence on the facts, then it is our duty to suspend judgment and hold no belief, just as definitely as it is our duty, when practical issues hang on our decision, not to suspend judgment, but to take our courage in both hands and act on the best belief to which we can arrive. This duty of refraining from belief is often imposed upon men of science in their work, in order that they may in the long run arrive at greater certitude; it is also imposed upon them in other cases in order that they may not encourage false hopes of certitude. When applied to whole problems, this attitude of mind generally goes by the name (first coined by Thomas Huxley) of Agnosticism. I hold it to be an important duty to know when to be agnostic. I believe that one should be agnostic when belief one way or the other is mere idle speculation, incapable of verification; when belief is merely held to gratify desires, however deep-seated, and not because it is forced on us by evidence; and when belief may be taken by others to be more firmly grounded than it really is, and so come to encourage false hopes or wrong attitudes of mind.

.   .   .   .   .

Now that all this has been said, the ground is clear for more definite statements. In the first place, I believe, not that there *is* nothing, for that I do not know, but that we quite assuredly at present *know* nothing beyond this world and natural experience. A personal god, be he Jehovah, or Allah, or Apollo, or Amen-Ra, or without name but simply God, I *know* nothing of. What is more, I am not merely agnostic on the subject. It seems to me quite clear that the idea of personality in God or in any super-natural being or beings has been put there by man, put into and round a perfectly real conception which we might continue to call God if the word had not acquired by long association the implication of a personal being; and therefore I disbelieve in a personal god [1] in any sense in which that phrase is ordinarily used.

For similar reasons, I disbelieve in the existence of Heaven or Hell in any conventional Christian sense. As for any pretended knowledge about the Last Judgment, or the conditions of existence in Purgatory, it could be disregarded as what it is, mythology from racial childhood, and left to die a natural death, if it did not require to be attacked as the too-frequent cause of unfortunate practical effects, such as causing believers to pay money to priests for the supposed benefit of souls in the other world.

As to the existence of another world or another life at all, there I am simply agnostic : I do not know. I find extreme difficulties, in the light of physio-

---

[1] Under the term *personal* god I include all ideas of a so-called superpersonal god, of the same spiritual and mental nature as a personality but on a higher level, or indeed any supernatural spiritual existence or force.

B

logical and psychological knowledge, in understanding how a soul could exist apart from a body;
but difficulties are never disproof. It also seems
clear enough that many ideas about a future life owe
their origin to the most primitive kinds of speculation and superstition among barbaric or savage races,
and have survived largely owing to man's enormous
conservatism in regard to tampering with what has
come to be regarded as sacred. Further, that many
other such ideas are merely the expression of man's
deep desire and longing for a continuation of life
after death for himself and for those he loves.

Finally, there is the so-called evidence from spiritualism. I have seen some of this, and read a good
deal on the subject; there seems to be a good *prima
facie* case for the existence of such " super-normal "
phenomena as clairvoyance and telepathy, as well as
plenty of undoubted automatic writing, hypnotic
phenomena, etc., but these have nothing to do with
spiritualism in the sense of communicating with the
spirits of the departed. The evidence for spiritualism
itself is for the most part so trivial that it is really
necessary to take part in a few séances to be able to
appreciate what childish and dubious phenomena
are uncritically accepted as evidence by believers.

I can hear many of my readers asking themselves
what then is left for me to believe in of anything
which can possibly be called religious. That such a
question can be asked is due to a misapprehension—
common enough, I admit, but none the less a misapprehension—as to the real nature and essence of
religion.

What, then, is religion? It is a way of life. It is a
way of life which follows necessarily from a man
holding certain things in reverence, from his feeling
and believing them to be sacred. And those things
which are held sacred by religion primarily concern
human destiny and the forces with which it comes
into contact.

I believe, then, that religion arose as a feeling of the sacred. The capacity for experiencing this feeling in relation to various objects and events seems to be a fundamental capacity of man, something given in and by the construction of the normal human mind, just as definitely as is the capacity for experiencing anger or admiration, sympathy or terror. What is more, we experience each of these feelings or sentiments in relation to certain general kinds of situations. There is no specific connection between any given object and a particular feeling, but there does exist one type of situation in which men tend to feel anger, another in which they tend to feel admiration, another in which they tend to feel reverence. But (and a very important *but*) in every case the type of situation which tends to arouse any particular feeling is always found to alter with experience and education. Many of the situations which arouse fear in a child cease to arouse fear when he has grown up; many situations which arouse fear in a young savage would not do so in a civilized child of the same age, and vice versa.

So it is with the religious feeling, the sentiment of sacredness. No one expects a child of four to have the same kind of religious life as a boy of sixteen, or either of them as a man of thirty. Nor should any one expect a savage to have arrived at the same religious attitude as a civilized man with different natural endowments and with centuries of developing tradition at his back. The situations which arouse the religious feeling cannot be expected to be the same in the various cases. This elementary truth has, however, not been grasped by many missionaries and missionary societies; and the failure to grasp it has often led to disastrous results.

The essential of all this, to my mind, is that religion is an activity of man which suffers change like all other human activities; that it may change for the better or for the worse; that if it stand still and refuse to change when other human activities are changing, then the standing still is itself a change for the worse; that as it grows it cannot avoid coming into contact both with intellectual and with moral or ethical problems; and that, with the development and broadening of human experience and tradition, religion becomes inevitably preoccupied with the intellectual comprehension of man's relation to the universe, and with the attainment of a coherent and unified moral life as well as with its more original quest for emotional satisfaction in the sphere of the holy. This emotional quest also shows a characteristic development. If at the outset it concerns itself mainly with putting man right with objects or beings regarded as endued with sacred power, and with the release of his perplexed spirit from the heavy burden of sacred awe, in later stages its most urgent desire is to gain the quality of holiness for the man himself, and to arrive by one road or another at an assurance of personal salvation. Finally, in its most developed and highest manifestations, this emotional side of the religious life aspires to a sense of communion with the divine, and to the peace and security which spring from the surrender of the individual will to what is usually described as the will of God.

It remains now for me to make, very briefly, some preliminary statement as to how I would interpret the religious view of God, since this, and all its corollaries, seems to me to be the one essential point of difference outstanding between " religion " and " science " to-day—religion in the sense not only of Christian orthodoxy but of all theism, and science not only in the sense of physics, chemistry, or biology, but of organized knowledge and thought based upon a naturalistic outlook.

Once adjust this difficulty, and there remains no conflict of principle. All the vital facts of religious life still remain; they but want re-defining in new terms. The living reality will need to change its clothes—that is all.

But meanwhile the difficulty is there; and it is a formidable one. Humanity in general, and religious humanity in particular, has for so long been habituated to thinking mainly in terms of an external, personal, supernatural, spiritual being, that it will indubitably be extremely difficult to abandon this view and see God as a creation of the human soul (albeit a necessary and fruitful one), compounded of the hard facts of soulless nature and the spiritual and intellectual aspirations of the nature of man, the two organized into a single whole by the organizing power of the human mind.

This same organizing power operates in other spheres, in the same way, and equally fruitfully—it can blend the hard facts of nature's chaos with its own spiritual aspiration for order, into the glorious achievement of a so-called Law of Nature; it can equally blend the hard facts of nature, including the humdrum and the tragic, with its own thoughts and its own aspirations for beauty, into that organized expression of experience which we call a work of art. In an almost more intimate way it can blend the hard facts of life and the aspirations of the human mind for happiness and virtue into the single organized whole which we call character.

Finally, the reconciliation between the two apparently conflicting aspects of life, the physical and the mental, is found in what may be regarded as the highest activity of all, namely the moulding of mere matter in conformity with mental experience—making matter express the vision of beauty, forcing the body to follow the physical or moral laws which the mind has perceived, utilizing the pure intellectual experience of the physicist and mathematician to control and harness natural forces in ways which neither nature herself nor human ignorance could do, making the material subserve the ideal. These achievements are represented by works of art, by moral and rational action, by machines like the dynamo or inventions like the aeroplane, by civilization in so far as it deserves its proud name.

On this view man's idea of God, and his expression of it, is on a par with his discovery and formulation of purely intellectual truth, his apprehension and expression of beauty, his perception and his practice of moral laws. There is no revelation concerned in it more than the revelation concerned in scientific discovery, no different kind of inspiration in the Bible from that in Shelley's poetry. That is to say that there is no literal revelation, no literal inspiration; and it is mere prevarication to shift, as is often done, from one sense of these words to the other, from the wholly literal, implying revelation or inspiration by supernatural beings, to the descriptive-metaphorical, implying only the flashing on to consciousness of something new, independent of the will, and carrying with it a quality of essential rightness.

But even if it should be admitted, as in point of fact it is admitted by an enlightened minority, that religious truth is never absolute, and must never be bound by the shackles of a pretended literal revelation, but is progressively discovered and built up, that would not bridge the gulf of which I have spoken. For it might be held (as it is by most of the enlightened minority in question) that it was a progressive discovery of the attributes and activities of a supernatural being.

What grounds are there for denying that this is so? They are numerous and complex, and can be fully appreciated only after some study of comparative religion and religious psychology. In this chapter I can do no more than state them baldly as I see them. In the first place comes the undoubted fact that man at most levels of culture has a strong penchant for personification. Primitive peoples personify all sorts of natural objects, and the same process continues into quite late stages of culture.

Together with the undoubted fact of wholesale personification in the earliest stages of human culture, there is the equally undoubted fact of the gradual limitation during historical time of the personifying tendency and its results. This occurs in three ways. On the one hand, as man perceives more clearly the connections between things and events, and comes to see more of the unity underlying the apparently disjointed chaos of phenomena, the number of separate personifications is reduced, but their scale or scope is correspondingly magnified. In the second place, their relation to material happenings is put more in the background : the personified sun, for instance, becomes a supernatural being who controls the sun, the sea envisaged as a god becomes the sea together with a god of the sea. And thirdly, their sphere of activity becomes curtailed. If the rainbow is generated by the refraction of the sun's rays on falling rain, it is not set in the sky as a sign by God. In short, if events are due to natural causes, they are not due to supernatural causes. Their ascription to supernatural beings is due merely to man's ignorance combined with his passion for some sort of " explanation " : they are myths—in other words, sacred versions of Just So Stories. For both these reasons we must at least be prepared to discount any statements made as to the existence of super-human persons.

There exists also a psychological reason to the same effect. Personality is the category most easily understood by man, since he himself has personality.

To those who approach the matter without any prepossessions as to the existence or non-existence of superhuman personal beings, and have taken the trouble to look into something of the history of religions and the workings of the human mind, it certainly seems as if this identical tendency towards personification had been at work throughout the whole gamut of gods, and that there is in this respect only a difference of degree between the simplest animism and the highest monotheism.

If we were prepared to admit that the ascription of personality or external spiritual being to gods were an illusion or an error, our comparison of religion with science or with art would then be complete. Each then would be a fusion of external fact with inner capacity into vital experience (or, looked at from a slightly different angle, each would be an expression of that vital experience). There does exist an outer ground and object of religion as much as an outer object for science. The fact, however, that this outer object is by most religions considered to be an external divine being is, philosophically speaking, an accident; it remains real whether so considered or not, just as the outer objects of science remain real whether we consider that laws of nature inhere in them or in the human mind. Not only so, but the ascription of personal being to religion's external object is best thought of as in origin a natural and inevitable error of primitive thinking, now surviving in highly modified form, a mistaken projection of personality into the non-personal.

If, however, this superposed belief and its corollaries be removed, what remains of the reality? The answer is " a great deal." That reality includes permanent facts of human existence—birth, marriage, reproduction, and death; suffering, mutual aid, conradeship, physical and moral growth. It includes also other facts which we may call the facts of the spiritual life, such as the conviction of sin, the desire for righteousness, the sense of absolution, the peace of communion; and those other facts, the existence and potency of human ideals, which, like truth and virtue and beauty, always transcend the concrete and always reveal further goals to the actual. It also includes facts and forces of nature outside and apart from man—the existence of matter and of myriads of other living beings, the position of man on a little planet of one of a million suns, the facts and laws of motion, matter, and energy and all their manifestations, the history of life. I say that it includes these; it would be more correct to say that it includes certain aspects of all these and many other facts. It includes them in their aspect of relatedness to human destiny; and it includes them as held together, against the cosmic background, by a spirit of awe or reverence. If you wish more precision, it includes them in their sacred aspect, or at least in association with an outlook which is reverent or finds holiness in reality.

Finally, it includes them, but not merely disjointedly, as so many separate items : it includes them in a more or less unified whole, as an organized scheme of thought; and as a matter of fact this scheme tends in its higher manifestations to be organized somewhat after the pattern in which a human personality is organized. It is this, among the other causes that have been mentioned, which helps to give this organized scheme of thought the illusion of possessing personality.

This organization of the external raw material into what is usually spoken of as the idea of God resembles closely the organization of external raw material by other human capacities into what are usually called Laws of Nature. Both are products of the human mind, but both have their external ground. However, the external ground of the idea of God differs from the external ground considered, for instance, by physico-chemical science, in being partly spiritual. In so far as it includes among the forces affecting human destiny the general ideals of humanity, even so far as it includes one's individual ideals (since those reach out far beyond the limits of personality), it includes spiritual realities.

This, be it noted, is a very different thing from saying that the ground of religious experience is wholly spiritual; or from asserting, with some philosophers, that the ground of all reality and existence is wholly spiritual, which hypothetical ground, then christened Absolute, is inserted from above through the philosophical trap-door as a substitute for the God built up by religion or by quite other methods and out of quite other aspects of reality. I feel strongly that this *deux ex machina* of certain philosophies is a dummy God, no more like the rich, vivid, and compelling experience of divinity which is enjoyed by many religious persons than is shadow like substance, or than is a formula like the reality which it partially represents.

For my own part, the sense of spiritual relief which comes from rejecting the idea of God as a supernatural being is enormous. I see no other way of bridging the gap between the religious and the scientific approach to reality. But if this rejection is once accomplished the abyss has disappeared in the twinkling of an eye, and yet all the vital realities of both sides are preserved. The mental life of humanity is no longer a civil war but a corporate civilization. Within it there will be conflicts, frictions, adjustments; but these are inevitable and probably necessary for full vitality, and if they take place within a whole which is organized for unity and production instead of duality and strife, there will be advance.

If religion be a way of life founded upon the apprehension of sacredness in existence; if, as is the case, the human consciousness be not satisfied with the mere experiencing of sacredness and mystery, but attempts to link this up with its faculty of reason and its desire for right action, trying on the one hand to comprehend the mystery and to explain the reality which it still feels sacred, and on the other to sanctify morality and make right action itself a sacrament; if this linking up of rational faculty and morality with the specifically religious experience of holiness has resulted in organizing the external ground of religion as what is usually called God; and if, finally, there be no reason for ascribing personality or pure spirituality to this God, but every reason against it : then religion becomes a natural and vital part of human existence, not a thing apart; a false dualism is overthrown; and the pursuit of the religious life is seen to resemble the pursuit of scientific truth or artistic expression, as one of the highest of human activities, success in which comes partly from native gifts, partly from early training and surroundings, partly from sheer chance, and partly from personal efforts.

I have sketched some of my ideas so far as I can see them run. Do not let it be supposed, however, that I have any illusions about their range or completeness. They represent to me merely a single step. We do not know what the future will bring forth. The visions of to-day may be the facts of to-morrow. I have no doubt that the advance of thought and discovery will reveal to us wholly undreamt-of facts concerning the nature of matter and its relation to mind or spirit ; when that happens, a new orientation of religious thought will be needful. Meanwhile the one main step that can be taken now, in the light of the present development of thought and knowledge, I have already laboured : it is the reform of theology on the three-fold basis of agnosticism, of evolutionary natural science, and of psychology.

CHAPTER II

A PRELIMINARY INTERPRETATION

There is little comfort in the assurance that science has been reconciled with religion unless the religion it has been reconciled with is a good religion.—Principal L. P. JACKS.

By the continual living activity of its non-rational elements a religion is guarded from passing into " rationalism." By being steeped in and saturated with rational elements it is guarded from sinking into fanaticism or mere mysticality, or at least from persisting in these, and is qualified to become a religion for all civilized humanity.—R. OTTO, *The Idea of the Holy*.

All problems of religion, ultimately, go back to this one :—the experience I have of God within myself differs from the knowledge concerning Him which I derive from the world. In the world He appears to me as the mysterious and marvellous creative Force; within me He reveals Himself as ethical Will. In the world He is impersonal Force; within me He reveals himself as Personality.—ALBERT SCHWEITZER, *Christianity and the Religions of the World* (1923).

The monotheist is apt to overprize the mere unity in his Ideal, forgetful that unity, if it grow too great, is tyrannous. . . . Indeed, more than once in history a divine unity and concord has been attained at a cost of human colour and the rich play of interest and feeling. . . . The Ideal is not merely a unity; it is quite as much a wealth and a diversity. So that Triune monotheism might be looked upon, perhaps, as a measure of religious self-protection. It is an anchor cast to windward, lest the drift toward unity wreck the very conception of the Ideal.—G. M. STRATTON, *Psychology of the Religious Life*.

He alone is the true atheist to whom the predicates of the Divine Being, for instance, love, wisdom, justice, are nothing.—FEUERBACH, *The Essence of Christianity*.

When their tabernacles are broken down, and the sun in his strength quells at last the unclean fumes of their censers and sacrifices, their eyes are blinded with that splendour, and they cry out that the world is darkened.—Sir FREDERICK POLLOCK.

There are Christians that place and desire all their happiness in another life, and there is another sort of Christians that desire happiness in this. . . . Not the vain happiness of this world, falsely called happiness, truly vain : but the real joy and glory of the blessed, which consisteth in the enjoyment of the whole world in communion with God; not this only, but the invisible and eternal, which they earnestly covet to enjoy immediately; for which reason they daily pray, Thy Kingdom come, and travail towards it by learning wisdom as fast as they can.

Whether the first sort be Christians indeed, look you to that. They have much to say for themselves. Yet certainly they that put off felicity with long delays are much to be suspected.—THOMAS TRAHERNE, *Centuries of Meditations*.

In this opposition between the essentially finalistic microcosm and the purely mechanical macrocosm lies the ultimate foundation of the age-long struggle between science and religion, the first constrained by reason founded on facts to deny finality [purpose] to the universe, the second urged irresistibly to affirm it by the imperious demands of feeling.—E. RIGNANO, in *Psyche* (1926).

IF what I have said in the preceding chapter is in principle correct, then current theology requires reinterpretation. It is also evident that many differences of detail would be possible in the interpretation, according both to the church or sect chosen and to the individual temperament of the interpreter. That elasticity of framework which has made it possible for Christianity to appeal to men of all grades of culture and to societies in all stages of development is one of the most notable facts about it. God the Father, for instance, must wear very different aspects to a Catholic mystic and a Hell-fire revivalist preacher.

But the broad outlines of the picture were drawn alike for all by the Council of Nicæa, when it laid down the doctrine of the Trinity with its three coequal persons. That doctrine, in spite of occasional intellectual revolts from its incomprehensibility, has appealed to the European mind for so many centuries that even the most bigoted opponent of Christianity would have to admit that the doctrine satisfies certain human needs and corresponds in some way with reality.

As I see it broadly, " God the Father " is a personification of the forces of non-human Nature; " God the Holy Ghost " represents abstract ideals; and " God the Son " personifies human nature at its highest, as actually incarnate in bodies and organized in minds, bridging the gulf between the other two, and between each of them and everyday human life. And the unity of the three persons as " One God " represents the fact that all these aspects of reality are inextricably connected.

The First Person of the Trinity, on this view, would be the theological name for the outer force and law which surround man whether he like it or not. There may be mind and spirit *behind* these powers, but there is none *in* them. The powers thus symbolized are strange, often seeming definitely alien to man and his desires, or even hostile. They go their ways inevitably, without regard for human emotions or wishes. They constitute the *mysterium tremendum* of religion. On the other hand, they are not always hostile or alien. The spring follows the winter; nature may bring the storm and the flood, but she also blesses with abundance; the powers of nature kill and terrify, but they also bring the sun to shine, the breeze to blow, and the birds to sing; they are powers of generation as well as of death.

In general, the forces and powers personified as the First Person are those which affect human life not only with their inevitability, but also with their quality of being entirely outside man. They may influence and subdue man, or man may influence and control them; they and man's mind may be fused in experience; but in themselves they are not only given, but external.

The realities symbolized in the Third Person of the Trinity, however, if my reading of theology is at all correct, are those which are equally given, but are, from the point of view of humanity as a whole, internal. From the point of view of the individual man, on the other hand, they have the peculiar quality of being felt as partly internal, immanent, belonging to the self; partly external, transcendent, and far greater than the personal self. They are ideals of value, and are inevitable to an organism which like man has reached the level of conceptual thought.

The rôle of different ideals within that sphere of reality which has been personified as the Holy Spirit has differed enormously in different ages and in different individuals and sects. It differs according to the scale of values which is adopted. In general, however, the ideals enshrined in the conception of the Holy Ghost include in the highest ranks those of righteousness with special reference to purity, and of truth with special reference to the sense of illumination, though they, of course, include many others as well. But it should not be supposed that the reality behind the Third Person of the Trinity consists solely of ideals. It includes also all those " winds of the spirit " which appear to come from some extra-personal region to fill the sails of the mind. We all know well enough that we may perceive an ideal, understand that it should be followed, and yet draw on no interior force which enables us to live by it or through it; and equally that we may be seized and possessed by spiritual forces which we do not recognize as having previously been part of our personality, uprushing we know not whence to drive us onwards in the service of some ideal. This, in some form or another, appears to be the almost universal experience of those who in obedience to their temperament and gifts have devoted themselves to pure art, pure science, pure philosophy, or pure religion : they seem when most successful in their work to be least personal.

The reality behind all these cases of irruptive spiritual force is constituted by those parts of the inborn capacities of mind and soul which have not been utilized in the building-up of personality.

The building-up of personality consists in adjusting the wholly or partially disconnected instincts and tendencies with which we are born, into a connected whole in which the parts are in organic relation with each ther; to this we are forced by experience, by the outer and inner conflicts which naturally occur but must be adjusted if we are to lead a life worth living, and by the light of reason which confronts the actual with the possible and the ideal.

This organized mutual relation of mental capacities and tendencies, each adjusted in some measure to the rest, and each thus becoming not merely one in a sum of properties, but an essential part of an organic unity, is what we call the personal self.

The other aspect of this problem to which I referred consists in the process, in a sense opposite to that we have just been considering, in which the personality, instead of adding to itself, has the sensation of being swallowed up in something larger than personality. This, however, will occur naturally whenever the pursuit of some ideal comes to dominate strongly over the immediate interests of the self.

In any case, in our attempt to translate the terms of Christian theology into terms of our own, we may say that what has been described as the Holy Spirit is that part of human nature which impresses by its givenness, by its transcendence of the personal self regarded as a self-centred mental organisation, and by its compulsive power of driving human nature on towards an ideal.

Finally there remains the Second Person, the Logos, the Son. In order not to be misinterpreted, let me remind my readers at the outset that orthodox theology, in regard to the Second Person of the Trinity, presents us with a doctrine far from simple, the result of a long process of development. The original idea of a temporal Messiah, destined in his lifetime to lead the chosen people to success, soon gave place to that of a Messiah shortly to come again in glory and bring the end of the world and the justification of the elect. As time went slowly by, and the Second Coming tarried, this idea too faded, and the messianic concept was transferred more and more to the kingdom that is within, to the problem of personal salvation. Here it made intimate contact with various of the existing mystery religions, which, long before the birth of Jesus, were built upon the idea of worshippers obtaining holiness through some form of mysterious communion with the god, and upon the possibility of transferring sacredness from god to man; Christianity both borrowed from and lent to these, on the whole receiving more than it gave. In the first few centuries of its existence it also made intimate contact with the Judaized Greek philosophy of which Philo is the most celebrated representative. Here it encountered the idea of the Logos, and eventually incorporated it, in a way peculiarly its own, with the messianic idea, both of course being linked up with the historical figure of Jesus. But even so, the doctrine of the Second Person was by no means established. As everyone who has an elementary acquaintance with Church history is aware, the full divinity of the Son—Messiah-Logos-Jesus—was long in dispute. For a large and important body, Christ was definitely less than divine, subordinate to God; and it was only after three centuries of theological dispute and development that the Council of Nicæa gave Christianity the doctrine of Christ as co-equal with God the Father, which it has retained with little or no modification to the present day.

When I speak of the Second Person of the Trinity,

c

therefore, I am not referring to the historical Jesus, nor to the idea of Jesus which was present to the minds of the twelve apostles or the early Church, but to this complex idea, as presented in the Nicene creed and subsequent theology, deriving from Jewish and pagan religious sources, from Greek philosophy, and from patristic theology, as well as from the man Jesus, the facts of his life and death, and the legends associated with him.

And this, I make bold to say, embodies the fundamental reality that only through human nature, through personalities with all their limitations, is the infinite of the ideal made finite and actual, is the potential which we have recognized behind the term Holy Spirit realized in the world, is the apparently complete discontinuity between matter and spirit bridged over. Modern science is able in one not unimportant particular to amplify the original doctrine. Through our knowledge of evolutionary biology we can see that human nature is not as a matter of fact alone in this; but that human nature merely does more efficiently, more completely, consciously, and on a definitely higher plane, what other life had been doing gropingly, unconsciously, and partially for æons before man ever was. We can therefore say that the nature which finds its highest expression in human nature constitutes this bridge; since, however, it is, so far as we know, human nature alone which mediates fully, or indeed at all in certain domains, between ideal and actual, between spiritual and material, it is human nature alone which need be fully considered, although the evolutionary background lends a richness and a solidity of foundation to all the conceptions involved.

This same conception, of human nature being in its highest aspects divine, is found in many places. It animates the myth of Prometheus who stole divine fire from heaven for man. It underlies the frequent deification, usually after death, of heroes and great men. It is at the root of Blake's allegorical mysticism, and of Wordsworth's famous "Ode." It made possible the existence and power of such ideas as the divine right of kings or the infallibility and supreme power of the popes as well as the actual deification and worship of the Roman Emperors during their lifetime.

To me it is simply the obverse of the ideas which have already been considered in relation to the Christian doctrine of the Holy Ghost. It is a matter of plain fact that all the faculties of human nature which seem most obviously immanent, yet possess in some degree the property of transcendence, in the same way in which the reverse was also found true. And this, as I have already tried to indicate, follows inevitably from the human faculty of conceptual thought, the concept always, by its mere nature, transcending every particular in the general, and automatically providing an ideal goal for every direction and every striving.

Orthodox theology, naturally moving within the bounds of the theistic conception, prefers to interpret these facts by saying that God was incarnated in human nature in the person of Jesus; and, when both liberal and logical, by admitting also that God is partially incarnated in all human beings.

I prefer to say that the spiritual elements which are usually styled divine are part and parcel of human nature. Thus the reality personified as the Second Person of the Trinity becomes to our reinterpretation the mediating faculty of human persons between the infinity of the ideal and the finite actuality of existence.

Finally, there remains the relation between the three persons of the Trinity—to us the three personifications of three aspects of reality.

In our task of re-interpretation we must ask what is the reality which is symbolized by the union of the three persons in one God. It is in this aspect of theology that I think the facts of science may be

seen to have the greatest value. Science has gone a
very long way towards proving the essential unity of all
phenomena. She has at least provided a strong basis
for a reasonable belief in this unity and continuity,
which, in the way in which it formulates itself to me
personally, I will do my best to summarize here.

I personally believe in the uniformity of nature—
in other words, that nature is seen to be orderly
once we take the trouble to find out the way of her
orderliness, and that there are not two realms of
reality, one natural, the other supernatural and from
time to time invading and altering the course of
events in the natural.

I believe also in the unity of nature. Scientific
discovery has tended without ceasing to reduce the
number of ultimate substances with which we have
to deal. There exist a million different species of
animals and plants, each chemically different from
the rest; each species contains thousands or millions
of chemically different individuals; there exist an
almost equally unlimited number of not-living,
separate and different substances of non-living
matter. Yet all these, alive or not, work with the
same energy, are built up out of the same matter,
resolvable into the same few score elements, and
these very elements in their turn (so the physicists
tell us) are merely so many different quantitative
arrangements of two kinds of units, of positive and
negative electricity. If the trend of discovery continues, we shall eventually be enabled to see these
positive and negative electricities as two modifications of the same final unitary substance.

I believe in unity by continuity. Matter does not
appear or disappear, nor do living things arise
except from previously existing things essentially
like themselves. The more complex matter that is
alive must at some time have originated from matter
that was not alive, but again by a gradual continuity, so that only by comparing the last stage

with the first could one see how considerable had
been the achievement. I believe in this continuity
of all matter, living or non-living; and I believe
also in the continuity of mind. If, as is the case,
mind and matter co-exist in the higher animals and
man; and if, as seems certain, the higher animals
and man are descended from lower animals, and
these in their turn from lifeless matter, then there
seems no escape from the belief that all reality has
both a material and a mental side, however rudi-
mentary and below the level of anything like our
consciousness that mental side may be.

In any case I believe in the unity of mind and
matter in the one ultimate world-substance, as two
of its aspects. Mental and material are thus, to my
belief, but two aspects of one reality, two abstractions
made by us from the concrete ground of experience;
they cannot really be separated, and it is false philosophy to try to think them apart.

These assurances of unity, uniformity, and continuity, derived from the discoveries of physico-
chemical science and evolutionary biology, were not
available to the intellectual enquirers of earlier ages,
who could thus only guess in the dark.

Utilizing these assurances as part of our background, we can then proceed to envisage the relation
between the three aspects of the unity of nature which
are symbolized as the three persons of the Trinity,
somewhat as follows. The First Person represents the
power and externality of matter and material law,
given and inexplicable. The Third Person represents
the illumination and compulsive power of thought,
feeling, will—the faculties of mind in its highest
ranges and at the level when it deals with universals;
these also are inexplicable, but must be accepted as
given. The Second Person is the link between the
other two; it is life in concrete actuality, mediating
between ideal and practice, incarnating (in perfectly
literal phrase) more and more of spirit in matter.

This progressive incarnation may be unconscious, as appears to be the case with organic evolution, or conscious, as in the deliberate attempt by man to realize his visions.

And all non-living nature is one matter; all life is constructed of and sprung from this same matter. Further, all thought and emotion, even the highest, springs from natural mind, whose slow development can be traced in life's evolution, so that life in general and man in particular are those parts of the world substance in which the latent mental properties are revealed to their fullest extent. Thus the three aspects of reality, so separate at first glance, are in point of fact genetically related in a single reality.

On the moral side too this unity underlying apparent diversity can also be traced. It may not solve the problem of evil, which is probably insoluble in the form in which it is usually stated, but it does contribute to the idea of a moral unity when it is found that movements and actions which at first sight seem neutral or evil are found on analysis to be inextricably part and parcel of a larger movement towards good. This is quite definitely so in regard to biological progress, and is also a commonplace of the human moralist.

.   .   .   .   .

I have in this chapter made some brief and extremely incomplete attempts at explaining the lines of thought that are in my mind, and at showing how certain ideas of current theology might be translated or interpreted in terms of this way of thinking. This must not be supposed to mean that I regard those doctrines of Christian theology, even when thus interpreted, as necessarily the best way of presenting the realities behind theology. The remaining part of the book will be largely taken up with justifying the line of approach which I have adopted, and in discussing possible ways of expressing religious realities.

CHAPTER III

THE SITUATION TO-DAY

Nowadays, matters of national defence, of politics, of religion, are still too important for knowledge, and remain subjects for certitude.—W. TROTTER, *Instincts of the Herd in Peace and War.*

The curious and sad fact is that the human mind seems to delight in creating prisons for itself. The scientific spirit created a mechanico-materialistic scheme which has ended by becoming the enemy of scientific research. And so with religion. The pride of a pretended knowledge reduces to a mechanical scheme the mysteries of life and death, and provides superficial standardised solutions for the problems of existence.—J. C. HARDWICK, *Religion and Science* (1920).

Though dogmas have their measure of truth, which is unalterable, in their precise forms they are narrow, limitative, and alterable : in effect untrue, when carried over beyond the proper scope of their utility. . . . In Christian history, the charge of idolatry has been bandied to and fro among rival theologians. Probably, if taken in its wide sense, it rests with equal truth on all the main churches, Protestant and Catholic. Idolatry is the necessary product of static dogmas. —A. N. WHITEHEAD, *Religion in the Making.*

We men of science, at any rate, hold ourselves morally bound to " try all things and hold fast to that which is good "; and among public benefactors, we reckon him who explodes old error, as next in rank to him who discovers new truth.—T. H. HUXLEY, *Life and Letters.*

Your astonishment at the life of fallacies, permit me to say, is shockingly unphysiological. They, like other low organisms, are independent of brains, and only wriggle the more, the more they are smitten on the place where the brains ought to be.—*Ibid.*

A practical man is a man who practises the errors of his forefathers.—BENJAMIN DISRAELI.

" The undevout astronomer is mad," said eighteenth-century deism; to-day we are more apt to think that the uncritical astronomer is dense. There is a sort of colossal stupidity about the stars in their courses that overpowers and disquiets us. . . . Consciousness itself is essentially greater than the very vastness which appals us, seeing that it embraces and envelops it.—WILLIAM ARCHER, *God and Mr. Wells* (1917).

One begins to wonder whether the material advantages of keeping business and religion in different compartments are sufficient to balance the moral disadvantages. The Protestant and Puritan could separate them comfortably because the first activity pertained to earth and the second to heaven, which was elsewhere. The believer in Progress could separate them comfortably because he regarded the first as the means to the establishment of heaven upon earth hereafter. But there is a third state of mind; . . . and if heaven is not elsewhere and not hereafter, it must be here and now or not at all. If there is no moral objective in Economic Progress, then it follows that we must not sacrifice, even for a day, moral to material advantage—in other words, that we may no longer keep business and religion in separate compartments of the soul.—J. M. KEYNES, in *The Nation and Athenæum* (1925).

Religion has lost the helm of the State, but not its own mystical power. It has turned inwards. There are more people interested in religion and more religious literature than ever before. Men are regular drunkards of the sacramental wines—in secret. Surrendering their outer lives to the State, they enthrone the Beloved Ego in their own hearts and worship him. . . . Since the State is separate from Religion, and Law from Morality, since Science is divorced from Wisdom, and Credit from real Service, men sever themselves from reality and try to dwell like Gods in their own imaginations. This is an intolerable life.—P. MAIRET, in *The New Age* (1927).

Mythology is the process of reflection which leads to conclusions eventually discarded as false, demonstrably false to any one who compared them with the idea of the Godhead which he had in his own soul. . . . The course of history has shown that religion could continue to exist after the destruction of mythology, as it had done after its birth. But of this the generations to whom myths had been transmitted and for whom mythology was the accepted page, could not be aware.—F. B. JEVONS, *The Idea of God* (1910).

WHAT is the situation to-day? It is common knowledge that the position of the established Christian churches and older sects is not what it was. Their own spokesmen lament the decay in the number of church members; the great falling-off in the matter of church-going; the corresponding spread of a purely irreligious spirit of mind, an untutored and unreflecting paganism veneered with jazz and motor-travel and wireless; the tendency to employ Sunday for general recreation rather than to regard it as a day of religious devotion; the dearth of candidates for the ministry, and, more serious still, dearth within dearth, the dearth of quality within the ranks of those who do present themselves; the extraordinary spread of mushroom faiths, crank beliefs, superstitions, new sects, and indeed new religions, of which the most important in numbers and influence are perhaps Christian Science and Spiritualism, although those which manage to combine what they are pleased to call New Thought with a flavour of Eastern religious thinking and philosophy, and also with some insistence upon vegetarianism or other unusual dietary, are serious rivals.

These are all grave changes for the older churches, and many of them, though by no means all (since desire for change in religious organization may denote a just dissatisfaction with the organizations existing at the time), are serious for religion as a whole, or at least for all the dominant creeds. But by far the gravest change of all is the abstention of a large part of the cultivated and disciplined thought of our time from all and sundry established or organized religions. This point hardly needs labouring; but it is so important and so serious that I must amplify it a little.

If there is one characteristic of our present age by which we may set it over against the Middle Ages, for example, or the Renaissance, it is the growth of scientific knowledge and scientific application. For six or seven centuries, ever since the scientific spirit began to raise its head after the supineness of the

Dark Ages, there has been intermittent friction or conflict between the Church and the scientific spirit. There was friction with some of the early anatomists; there was coercion of poor Roger Bacon, that genius born before his time; there was open conflict with Galileo over the question of the earth's central position in the scheme of things; there would have been conflict with Descartes had not that prudent man, with Galileo's fate before him, decided not to publish his cosmology; there was conflict with Giordano Bruno—conflict which ended in his being burnt alive; there was a great pother about William Smith and Lyell and the other early geologists when they showed that the Mosaic accounts of creation and of the deluge were untenable; there was (and still is) conflict with Darwin and his followers for maintaining the mutability of species and (most heinous crime of all!) for showing that man is descended by natural evolution from lower animals; there was a great outcry when scientific method was applied, in the form of the so-called " Higher Criticism," to the text and sources of the Bible, and especially the Gospels; there is to-day friction, though of a confused sort, between the usual Christian view and the discoveries of modern psychology.

Those struggles of the nineteenth century terminated by the leaders of religious thought climbing down from their fathers' untenable position and using the discoveries of science—so recently abominated—to buttress their own new-modified views. This climbing-down process, however, went so far that the position of the more liberal-minded Christians became vague and indeed equivocal. By some schools of liberal theology the Mosaic account of creation and of the fall of man is not literally believed in, but upheld as symbolic or dismissed as myth. The more flagrant miracles of both Old and New Testament are discounted as inventions of a credulous age, while the rest can be set down to faith-healing.

As regards more general principles, the change is equally radical. The liberal theologian, believing in the uniformity of nature and recognizing the validity of the laws of nature as revealed by the patient testing of science, inevitably finds the activities of his personal God receding more and more into the background. God does not make the rivers burst out in flood, or release the lightning, or cause the earthquake or the epidemic, in the simple and direct causal and personal way which was originally believed. If he causes them, it is in no other way than that in which all events in the world, from the fall of a stone or the boiling of a kettle, are caused : in other words, liberal theology is thus being driven either into the unsatisfactory unorthodoxy of pure pantheism, or else to belief in a God in some way wholly outside or behind the world of existence, who perhaps has set the machinery going, but does not any longer interfere with it, and in any event is thus become much more shadowy, far, and remote than the God of the Middle Ages.

The result, to one observing it dispassionately, appears to be an unsatisfactory mixture. The two components refuse to interpenetrate or combine, and the main effect is a dilution of both. The theistic view has been watered down and lost much of its power and savour ; the scientific outlook is not rigorously adhered to, and so loses the severity and compelling force which is one of its great sources of strength.

One of the most urgent needs of humanity at the present time is a common outlook, comparable in its comprehensiveness and wide acceptance with the common outlook, religious and philosophical, which dominated the Middle Ages. Even during the Roman Empire there can scarcely have existed such diversity of incompatible systems of thought, all claiming the complete allegiance of men, as exists to-day.

The world is very much in the melting-pot; and it will not be able to jump out until it knows in what direction it wants to jump. But to know this it must have some clear general ideas in its head, not be fed with incompatible notions until it feels bewildered and gives up any attempt at comprehension. Neither existing religion nor existing science is equal to the task. All the great religions of the present stick tight to doctrines which science and any educated thought which takes account of science finds difficult or impossible of acceptance. Science, being yet young and having naturally set out to grapple with the simpler facts of nature, is well organized only on the side of physics, chemistry, and pure biology; on the human side, with its incredible complexities and its great diversities of individual minds, it is yet infantile, and we can still learn much more about some aspects of human nature from poets and novelists, from looking at pictures and listening to music, from a study of religion and mysticism, from history and biography, not to mention from daily intercourse, than from all the text-books of psychology in existence.

Is it perhaps the fact that religion, firmly based in actuality of emotion and experience, but feeling the absolute need of some intellectual explanation, has invented an *ad hoc* explanation, satisfactory enough as provisional hypothesis, but which she has afterwards made the grave mistake of setting up as immutable truth? Is it perhaps the fact that, on the other hand, science, secure in her firm grounding, has made the error of thinking that destruction of the intellectual scaffoldings of religion would impair the reality of religion itself?

If that be true—and the rest of this book will be largely an attempt to prove it so—then the chief task of religion in helping to build up the unified thought of the future is to abandon the intellectual arrogance of its theology and to take a leaf out of the book of science as to the methods by which truth may best be pursued; while the chief task of organized science in the same quest will be to enlarge its bounds, admit that the highest flights of the human spirit are as much realities as the routine activities of the human body or the doings of the atoms and molecules of lifeless matter, to recognize for what they are the realities on which the religious life is based, to see religion's values.

CHAPTER IV

SOME FUNDAMENTALS

Our age is retrospective. It builds the sepulchres of the fathers. . . . Why should not we also enjoy an original relation to the universe? Why should not we have a poetry and philosophy of insight and not of tradition, and a religion by revelation to us, and not the history of theirs? . . . The sun shines to-day also. There is more wool and flax in the fields. Let us demand our own works, and laws, and worship.—RALPH WALDO EMERSON, *Essays.*

Whatever the world thinks, he who hath not much meditated upon God, the human mind, and the *summum bonum*, may possibly make a thriving earthworm, but will most indubitably make a sorry patriot and a sorry statesman.— Bishop BERKELEY, *Siris.*

Incomprehensible? But because you cannot understand a thing, it does not cease to exist.—PASCAL, *Pensées.*

When we review the various forms in which men think of divinity and express their reverence, we involuntarily ask, " Which of these is better, and which worse? " . . . An effort should be made, perhaps, not so much to give a definite and direct answer to the question, as to offer some of the standards for judging rival forms of religion. . . . First would come this, that *the pure and continued expression of any single religious motive is undesirable.* For, indeed, religious motives, like muscles, work best in opposition. . . . Yet such a thought should be supplemented at once, inasmuch as while retaining each and both of two opposing motives, *one motive may well be dominant.* . . . The supreme virtue of thought, however, is not its balance and vigour and richness, but its veracity. Accordingly a third rule to guide our judgment may be that *the assertions of religion, as to what is real, should be true.* And this at once brings us to a distant region where we are met by Pilate's question; and also by the thought that it is not the office of religion to *know*, but only to be loyal, that if there be avenues to truth, they lie not in religion, but in science and philosophy.—G. M. STRATTON, *Psychology of the Religious Life.*

Common sense and a respect for realities are not less graces of the spirit than moral zeal. . . .

. . . They [the Nonconformist Churches] saw the world of business and society as a battlefield, across which character could march triumphant to its goal, not as crude materials waiting the architect's hand to set them in their place as the foundations of the Kingdom of Heaven. It did not occur to them that character is social, and society, since it is the expression of character, spiritual. Thus the eye is sometimes blinded by light itself.—R. H. TAWNEY, *The Rise of Capitalism* (1926).

Like the celestial order, of which it is the dim reflection, society is stable, because it is straining upwards.—R. H. TAWNEY (on the mediæval religious view), *Ibid.*

In so far as it knows the eternity of truth and is absorbed in it, the mind *lives* in that eternity. In caring only for the eternal, it has ceased to care for that part of itself which can die.—GEORGE SANTAYANA, *The Ethics of Spinoza.*

IT is my next task to attempt some account of the realities on which religion is based. Obviously, this task is much the most difficult which I shall have to undertake. But, however difficult, the task must be undertaken. It can only be even approximately successful if reader co-operates with writer by the goodwill of sympathetic imagination. So I must ask that my readers take for granted my sincerity, my desire to reach beyond the appearances of the surface to realities below, and an absence of any wish to make debating points or to score a barren victory of mere argument.

It is often stated that the essential of religion is belief in God, meaning by that in a personal or superpersonal Divine being, or at least a belief in supernatural Beings of some kind. This, however, is manifestly not true. There are whole religions which make no mention of God. The most notable example is that of Buddhism in its pure and original form. Not only that, but even in countries where a theistic religion is current, and even among the most devoted adherents of such religions, there exist, normally and regularly, acts and thoughts and experiences which most certainly must be called religious, but which equally certainly do not of themselves demand explanation in terms of God.

I propose therefore to leave the idea of God on one side for the present, as an interpretation or explanation by theology of certain ultimate and irreducible facts which we may call the facts of religious experience. Let it not be forgotten that our knowledge of the thoughts and inner nature of other men and women, even of those who are nearest to us, is indirect, an interpretation or explanation of their actions, of their expression, of the arbitrary symbols called words which they employ. We know directly no human consciousness save our own.[1] Thus if, in common with liberal thinkers within the churches, we reject the idea of direct revelation as merely the crude symbolism of an earlier age, our simplest and most direct idea or experience of God will also involve an interpretation, and a very much more difficult and indirect one than that by which we recognize the existence of minds in our fellow-men. It will be an interpretation of facts of outer nature and of the human spirit and its experiences.

One further small digression before coming to the main subject of this chapter, a digression upon symbolism. In matters of religion, symbols have always played a considerable part. The man of science and the pure intellectualist will see in this a foolishness which may become dangerous. He is right about its possible danger. Symbols are, unfortunately, often

[1] The only possible way in which direct experience of another's consciousness could occur would be by means of telepathy, should this be proved to exist. Those who assert that we can have a direct intuition of others' personality, apparently not by means of telepathy (*e.g.*, Baron von Hügel), are simply misusing the term and mistaking the faculty of intuition, which is a marvellously speedy and unitary interpretation, for a non-interpretative faculty, mystical in its nature, of direct knowledge.

mistaken for reality. Conclusions are then drawn from this supposed reality, and these conclusions may involve the performance of actions which may be merely laughable (or pitiable—so often the same thing!) in the eye of later reason, or, too often, tragic or cruel. Human sacrifice is perfectly logical if you believe that God is a being who can provide victory if propitiated, and who delights in the death of human victims as a propitiation : but if you have merely symbolized your own low level of moral outlook by ascribing to your god such bloody-minded mercenariness, then your human sacrifice is, in spite of your sincerity, a crime. The cross is naturally the central symbol of Christianity; but to believe that the sign of the cross will frighten away devils or evil-minded persons, or that a fragment of the true cross could have power to bring miracles to pass, is folly and superstition arising from mistaking the symbol for the sacred power symbolized. None the less, symbolism plays a legitimate and even necessary part in religion.

We now approach the crux of the matter—namely, the question of the reality at the basis of religion. In attacking this question it will be of service to pass in review a few definitions of religion.

There have been many attempts to define religion ; and the number of definitions produced is almost as great as the number of men who have attempted definition. What is more, many of the definitions are mutually contradictory, and many seem to have no common ground at all with others.

Matthew Arnold defined religion as " morality tinged with emotion." Salomon Reinach, that learned and sceptical French Jew, calls it "a body of scruples which impede the free exercise of our faculties." Professor E. B. Tylor proposes " the belief in spiritual beings " as what he calls a minimum definition of religions.

Max Müller, on the other hand, preferred to say

D

that " Religion consists in the perception of the
infinite under such manifestations as are able to influence the moral character of man." Sir James
Frazer, who has perhaps done as much as any single
man since Darwin to change the thought of the
world, seeks his definition along wholly different
lines. He says that religion is " a propitiation or
conciliation of powers [which he elsewhere defines
as ' conscious or personal agents '] superior to man,
which are believed to direct and control the course
of nature and of human life." Jevons in his *Idea of
God* says " the many different forms of religion are
all attempts to give expression to the idea of God."
It should be noted, however, that Jevons is willing
to extend the idea of God to cover the numerous
spirits of the animistic stage of religion, and even
fetishes.

In a recent book Professor Whitehead, who embodies in his one person the rare combination of
philosopher, man of science, man of letters, and
mathematician, has given us (in spite of great ob-
scurity in his main construction and in his philo-
sophic approach to theology) some illuminating
phrases on religion. As a preliminary to definition,
he contrasts human activities such as arithmetic
with religion. " You *use* arithmetic, but *you* are
religious." He then goes on to say that " Religion
is force of belief cleansing the inward parts. . . .
A religion, on its doctrinal sides, can thus be described as a system of general truths which have
the effect of transforming character when they are
sincerely held and vividly apprehended."

T. H. Huxley, after speaking of " the engagement
of the affections in favour of that particular kind of
conduct which we call good," continues, " I cannot
but think that it, together with the awe and reverence, which have no kinship with base fear, but
arise whenever one tries to pierce below the surface
of things, whether they be material or spiritual,

constitutes all that has any unchangeable reality in religion." This by its form does not claim to be a general definition : but it is interesting as one of the earlier attempts at psychological clarification.

These examples could be multiplied : but they will have served to show what diversity of thought exists on the subject. All the definitions so far given are incomplete, emphasizing one aspect of religion to the exclusion of others. But the essential religious reality, the experience which seeks to embody itself in symbols and to find intellectual expression in theologies—what is it? Is it not the sense of sacredness? And is not this sense of sacredness, like the feeling of hunger or the emotion of anger or the passion of love, something irreducible, itself and nothing else, only to be communicated to others who have the same capacity, just as the sensation of colour is incommunicable to a blind man? [1]

As Estlin Carpenter says : " An encyclopædic account, however, should rest rather on an exterior definition which can serve as it were to pigeon-hole the whole mass of significant facts. Such an exterior definition is suggested by M. E. Crawley in *The Tree of Life*, where he points out that neither the Greek nor the Latin language has any comprehensive term for religion, except in the one ἱερά, and in the other *sacra*, words which are equivalent to ' sacred ' "; and he concludes, " we may define, then, the religious object as the sacred."

This central, psychological definition has been adopted, with various modifications, by a number of writers, such as the Swedish Archbishop Söderbolm and the American anthropologist Lowie, by Dr R. R. Marett, and Dr Rudolf Otto. I can best amplify the conception by quoting from these last two authors.

Dr Marett, surveying the religions of primitive

[1] In modern psychological parlance this " sense " or " feeling " should be called a *sentiment*.

peoples with the dispassionate gaze of an anthropologist, writes as follows : " We must admit that in response to, or at any rate in connection with, the emotions of Awe, Wonder, and the like, wherein feeling would seem for the time being to have outstripped the power of 'natural,' that is reasonable, explanation, there arises in the region of human thought a powerful impulse to objectify and even personify the mysterious or 'supernatural' something felt, and in the region of will a corresponding impulse to render it innocuous, or better still propitious, by force of constraint, communion, or conciliation."

Dr Otto is a well-known German Protestant theologian, whose book, *The Idea of the Holy*, was acknowledged in theological circles to be of first-rate importance. He finds in the direct experience of the holy in events, persons, things, and thoughts, not only the origin of religious feeling and beliefs in the past of primitive tribes, but the kernel of all that is of value in modern Christianity, as elsewhere in the religious life. He points out with some emphasis, not only that sacredness is in its origin quite remote from any moral associations or intellectual interpretations, but that even in developed religions, like Christianity, in which morality and intellect have come into close connection with religious feeling, the experience of sacredness is something *sui generis*, a direct experience like that of beauty or logical correctness, and that to substitute for it a rational moral feeling or an intellectual theological comprehension is to rob religious experience of its central core and religious feeling of its well-spring.

Speaking of this feeling in a developed religious consciousness, he writes : " Let us consider the deepest and most fundamental element in all strong and sincerely felt religious emotion. Faith unto Salvation, Trust, Love—all these are there. But over and above these is an element which may also on occasion, quite apart from them, profoundly affect us and occupy the mind with a well-nigh bewildering strength. Let us follow it up with every effort of sympathy and imaginative intuition wherever it is to be found, in the lives of those around us, in sudden, strong ebullitions of personal piety, . . . in the fixed and ordered solemnities of rites and liturgies, and again in the atmosphere that clings to old religious monuments and buildings, to temples and to churches. If we do so we shall find we are dealing with something for which there is only one appropriate expression, *mysterium tremendum*. The feeling of it may at times come sweeping like a gentle tide, pervading the mind with a tranquil mood of deepest worship. It may pass over into a more set and lasting attitude of the soul, . . . until at last it dies away and the soul resumes its ' profane,' non-religious mood of everyday experience. It may burst in sudden eruption up from the depths of the soul with spasms and convulsions, or lead to the strangest excitements, to intoxicated frenzy, to transport, and to ecstasy. It has its wild and demoniac forms and can sink to an almost grisly horror and shuddering. It has its crude, barbaric antecedents and early manifestations, and again it may be developed into something beautiful, pure, and glorious. It may become the hushed, trembling, and speechless humility of the creature in the presence of—whom or what? In the presence of that which is a *Mystery* inexpressible and above all creatures." I have quoted from Otto at some length, because I both the non-rational fact of religious experience and its psychological basis are so clearly put.

The power which religious feeling has to transform life is also vividly stated (though not perhaps so vividly as by Victor Hugo when, in *Les Misérables*, he wrote of the old housekeeper Mme. Baptistine, " Nature had created her merely a sheep; religion had transformed her into an angel ").

But this feeling, and the supernatural power which is assumed to explain it, are not necessarily good. The actual feeling, the " religious thrill," to borrow Lowie's phrase, is morally quite neutral, and, as Otto points out, may be debased or refined, experienced in relation to things in themselves either evil or good. And the supernatural power assumed to reside in objects thus felt sacred, the " theoplasm " of which gods are later made, is supposed to manifest itself for evil as well as for good ends, to be utilisable for black magic as well as for promoting fertility, to cause plagues and catastrophes as well as human blessings, to be the wrath of God as well as his love.

For this reason Marett prefers not to call what is experienced " the sacred " or " the holy," since these to us almost invariably connote only goodness, but to borrow the Polynesian word *Mana*, which is actually employed to-day to denote the mysterious power assumed to be resident in all objects, good or evil, desirable or to be shunned, which arouse this *awe-ful* sense. In the same way Otto feels constrained to coin a word for the experience of sacredness, and uses *numinous*, from the Latin *numen*, a divinity to be worshipped. It is not without significance that these similar results should have been reached by two very different minds, approaching the subject by wholly different routes.

One thing is clear from my list of definitions, that religious feeling and action and belief must be, or at least usually are, involved in religion. But without the aid of the psychological key provided by the definitions of Crawley, Marett, and Otto, it would be extremely difficult to see how these three components —emotional, practical, and intellectual—were fitted together in religion, and what common component of all religions there might be to which the term religious could be applied. What makes religious emotion religious and not merely æsthetic? What makes us say that one motive or reaction is religious, another moral? What is it that brings one piece of ceremonial or ritual within the pale of religion and leaves another outside? Why is it that we call one belief scientific and another religious?

We may put it in this way. The normal man has an innate capacity for experiencing sanctity in certain events, just as (on a lower and more determinate plane) he has for experiencing red or blue, fear or disgust or desire, or as he has for experiencing beauty, or the validity of logical proof, or for feeling love or hate, or judging good and evil. Some have this in an overmastering degree, and will be haunted all their days by their experiences of holiness and the felt need of conforming their life to them. The majority, on the other hand, have it much less intensely. They will, in their degree, understand holiness when it is pointed out to them, but be incapable of the pioneering discoveries or the power of expression of the exceptional few. These few are like the few creators in the world of poetry or music, the rest are like those who can and do respond to the creation of the poets and musicians and value it, while themselves remaining dumb. Finally, there are undoubtedly some who, either congenitally or through their upbringing, are wholly unable to appreciate what is meant by the sacred or the holy, just as there are a few men who are incapable of appreciating music, a few who are born with defect of the retina leading to colour-blindness, a few who are born imbecile, unable to follow a logical chain of reasoning, a few born moral imbeciles, incapable of appreciating what is meant by right or wrong, and many more in whom upbringing or their own mode of life has deadened or wholly distorted this moral sense.

Not only does the normal man have this capacity for experiencing the sense of the sacred, but he demands its satisfaction. This may come through the services of an organized church, as is shown by

the Russian peasants who in many places insisted on
building new churches in place of those that official
Bolshevism had destroyed or turned to other uses;
or through artistic expression; or through a religi-
ously-felt morality, the necessity of which to some
minds has been so finely put in *Romola* by George
Eliot that I cannot forbear from quoting: " The
highest sort of happiness often brings so much pain
with it, that we can only tell it from pain by its being
what we would choose before everything else, because
our souls see it is good."

I use the term " sense of the sacred " or " sense of
the holy " for want of a better. Had it not been
overlain by all sorts of alien and irrelevant ideas,
religious sense or *sentiment* would have been preferable.

The sense of the holy is a highly complex frame of
mind. One of its chief psychological accompaniments is awe, which is itself complex, with fear,
wonder, and admiration all entering into it as ingredients. Reverence, into which there also enters
submissiveness as an element, is a frequent if by no
means invariable accompaniment. But mystery may
probably be regarded as its real essence, with awe
as necessary, and reverence as common, ingredient.
The mystery may be merely the vulgar mystery of the
unusual or strange. The mysteriousness of this may
be wholly removed by education and knowledge.
But, be it noted, comprehension, in the ordinary
sense of understanding the past causal sequence by
which such and such an event or organism came into
existence, or of analysis of event or organism into its
component parts, with an understanding of how they
work—this does not by any means necessarily rob the
being or thing considered of mystery; but now it is a
mystery which no longer appeals to the untrained but
only to the educated sense.

Another characteristic of the sense of mystery in
the disciplined mind is that it tends to find its objects

more and more in the familiar, less in the merely unusual. This, too, has its parallel in art. It is only a temporary and uncompleted phase of art which gives us programme-music, subject-pictures, the purely narrative poem or story, the building which is striking at all costs. The great artist can make a kitchen table contain more beauty and meaning than a second-rate hand can infuse into a picture of the greatest event in history; and the finest works of art deal often with the simplest and most familiar human verities.

So with religion. The gaping spirit which needs to be stimulated by extravagance, miracle, or catastrophe, gives place to the insight which finds in the commonest facts material for reverence, wonder, or love.

When the fact of existence has become itself a wonder, there is no room for miracle in the vulgar sense.

There is still another point in which religion resembles art : good intentions are not enough. A man with a good natural taste, or with one that has been well trained and disciplined, will find certain attempts at artistic expression definitely *wrong*; they are to him not merely crude or immature or incomplete—those qualities can be readily forgiven—but they arouse in him a definite feeling of hostility or distaste owing to their stressing the lower at the expense of the higher, or distorting the whole scheme of values so as to become, to him, without value or even with negative value. When sickly sentiment takes the place of genuine feeling, when vulgarity takes the place of humour, when unreal motives are exalted at the expense of the strong reality of every day—then the result is intolerable to the man who knows better, in the same sort of way as it is intolerable to hear or see something which to us is supremely valuable greeted with a snigger or a leer.

Similarly, there are some whole religions, as well

as the religious views of many individual persons, to which the man who is acute or sensitive in his religious perceptions and emotions reacts simply by a feeling of repulsion, so incongruous or so pretentious do they appear.

Precisely the same is true of their moral aspect; and no amount of sincerity can condone, to those who have higher standards, the sanctification of evil through religion. For one or other of these reasons, many religions and religious actions are bound to seem repulsive or wicked to the developed religious consciousness. Nothing can make the religious sacrifice of human beings by the Aztecs seem anything but evil to us. We are filled with horror when we find that they took pleasure in representing, in their sacred art, the victim biting clean through his tongue in the moment of agony, presumably since the greater the pain of the victim the more would the god appreciate the sacrifice. On the other side, those who feel anything of the austerity of religion cannot but look with active distaste at the deliberate cultivation, by certain representatives of certain Christian bodies, of a religiosity of sentiment, especially among emotional women, which takes the undisciplined overflow of adolescence and sexual feeling, directs it on to religious objects, and in so doing not only encourages morbidity but degrades the objects of worship themselves.

· · · · ·

The chief ways in which religion has been moulded seem to be somewhat as follows.

In the first place, man demands some sort of explanation of the world and of his place in it. He dislikes to leave a mystery completely unexplained, though he rather prefers leaving it with some mysteriousness, and not wholly explained in a banal way. His attempts at intellectual explanation of facts which give rise to religious feeling are theology.

Originally these attempts are either crude rational-
izations or else myths—in other words, they are
attempts to provide rational support for a desire
without having real evidence or reasons at hand.
In the case of myths, the desire is primarily the desire
for explanation itself; to this there may also be
added the desire to explain in terms which gratify
other desires, such as that for immortality. Logic
and experience both then set to work on these " explanations," and proceed to improve them. Logic
improves by attempting to make them more complete, by trying to remove inherent contradictions;
experience tries to mould the explanations into
greater conformity with observed facts.

The sense of the sacred is only the root of the
matter. Religion as it developed—perhaps even
from the first—has involved intellect and morals and
ritual as well as feeling. Further, it has attached its
feeling of sacredness to all sorts of objects and ideas.

Logic and experience do not always tend in the
same direction, since logic will very often take certain premises for granted as self-evident (e.g., that a
personal god exists) and then draw conclusions from
them. The conclusions may bear no relation to
facts, or may even contradict experience; but such
conclusions of logic are often preferred by humanity
to the conclusions of experience.

One process which from the beginning makes
itself felt is the transference of the feeling of sanctity
experienced in relation to certain objects or events,
to the explanation later advanced to account for the
objects or events. This is due to the principle of
association so fundamental in the human mind.
So theology becomes sacrosanct, taboo to altera-
tions, in a way not found with scientific doctrines.
This accounts for the fact that there is such irrational
but strong resistance, on the part of religious people,
to theological changes: the proposals made are not
weighed on their intellectual merits, but are met by a

current of feeling. In addition, the force of authority is introduced. This comes about in two ways. For one thing, the mere fact of immemorial tradition becomes in itself sacred, and the fact that things have been done in one particular way for generations in the past becomes a valid reason for continuing to do so in the present and the future. And, secondly, the desire for reinforcing the sanctity of beliefs lead frequently to the assertion that they have been revealed, directly or indirectly, by supernatural authority. Religious conservatism is thus aided both by the authority of tradition and by that of revelation.

The foregoing shows how two separate bodies of explanation of phenomena can grow up side by side —theology and natural science. The one has grown up round objects experienced as sacred; the other has grown up round common objects, not regarded as worth consideration by religious intellects. But, unfortunately, explanations cannot be kept to localized regions of reality. Conclusions drawn from sacred science or theology overflow into everyday life and demand application to quite ordinary objects, while natural science, pursuing its humdrum methods, eventually comes to apply them to objects regarded as sacred as well as to ordinary ones.

It is thus probable that in the development of civilizations there will always come a time when science and theology will find themselves in conflict. Science and theology start in different regions of experience; the men who pursue the one are generally of very distinct type from the devotees of the other; and the emotional backgrounds of the two are quite different. But they inevitably grow, and therefore inevitably invade each other's territory. The only possible solution, save an indefinite prolongation of the conflict, is for religion to admit the intellectual methods of science to be as valid in theology as everywhere else, while science admits the psychological basis of religion as an ultimate fact.

The first point we have made is that the process of association can and does bring intellectual explanation, or at least certain attempts at a certain kind of intellectual explanation, into connection with religion, and so causes these explanations to become invested with the specific religious quality of sanctity.

In precisely the same way moral ideas can and do become linked by association with religion, and therefore sacred. Morals appear to acquire religious associations in several separate ways. In the first place the " negative sacredness," of which taboo is the developed form, becomes directly attached to actions which are found to shock one's own feelings or those of the community; these will include actions calculated to disturb any accepted sense of sacredness, like laughing in church, or quarrelling at a graveside; and also actions which run counter to the accepted standards of the community, as when a member of a warlike tribe shows cowardice, a member of a respectable Puritan family obtains a divorce, or a member of an aristocratic clan, in the far-off days before the last war, expressed a desire to become an actor or a professional violinist.

Thus a great deal of what we may call tribal morality and custom, merely for the reason that it is generally accepted, traditional, and prescribed by authority rather than reason, comes to have a certain religious sanctity attached to it, although without necessarily being thought of as having any connection with supernatural beings.

Meanwhile, however, the belief in supernatural beings is in existence. If they exist as personalities in any way like us, they too must have their morality —it is they who are responsible for the governance of the world, they who cause events to take place in accordance with their wishes.

The more man's reason gets to work on his religious problems, the more difficult does he find it to ascribe low moral insight and motives to his Gods.

At any particular time in history the moral character of his Gods comes largely to reflect his own moral ideas; but various peculiarities are added. Logic gradually compels the idea that the moral, like the intellectual and other qualities of God, are absolute and complete—that God is not only more powerful, better, and possessed of more knowledge than we, but all-knowing, omnipotent, and absolutely good. On the other hand, evil exists; and its existence is a challenge to the moral character of God. Two tendencies have, as a matter of fact, resulted from these two aspects of the problem. Either man, in his theology, prefers to see a God of absolute good perpetually in conflict with a Devil or supernatural being of evil nature; or else (which better satisfies the desire for logical unity), he ascribes to God wisdom and kindness infinitely transcending our own, so that evil of all sorts, including pain and misfortune, but especially moral evil, which seems so intolerable to us and so repugnant to our moral sense, is to God's absolute knowledge a necessity for our spiritual development, to his transcendent wisdom an obligatory move in the working out of the cosmic plan.

It has frequently been maintained that religious belief is needed as a buttress to both private and still more to public morality. Matthew Hales, a noted judge at the close of the seventeenth century, could write: "To say that religion is a cheat is to dissolve all those obligations whereby civil societies are preserved."

This idea has been, however, so often exploded that it is not worth while slaying the slain and going over once more the ground so well covered by Lecky, Westermarck, and others. I will content myself by quoting E. S. P. Haynes's dictum, that "if morality did really depend on other-worldly sanctions, the religious changes of the last fifty years would by now have dissolved society at large." But apropos of the question of divine personality it is worth while recalling, with Santayana, that "what makes for righteousness, the conditions of successful living, need not be moral in a personal sense, any more than the conditions of a flame need be themselves on fire." And let us also remember that the undue association of morals with religion has tended to surround morality with such a coat of untouchable sanctity that too often moral progress has for this very reason been much slower than might otherwise have been the case.

The final upshot is a compromise. By the time morals begin to be thought about instead of accepted as necessary tradition, the idea of a supernatural being in control of religious affairs has come into being. Logic, applied to man's developing moral sense, tends to make this supernatural being a model of moral perfection. On the other hand the facts of life, including the problem of evil, had long previously claimed attention and demanded, if possible, some explanation; and various theological myths had been invented for this purpose. Very frequently these myths involve actions or ideas of deity which are hardly consistent with a more developed morality. In these cases there is a cleavage between two views of God, a logical and moral difficulty which is sometimes openly acknowledged and discussed, more often simply slurred over. In the Book of Job the difficulty is faced. It is the problem of evil in its simplest form, in the form in which it haunted the practical mind of the early Hebrew, set upon this life rather than the next, upon national success and survival rather than any personal immortality Why do the wicked prosper, wax fat, and kick; why do misfortunes fall upon the innocent or those who have done their best to be upright? Job poses the question as applied to his own plight. His three friends answer, with the simple but crude faith which believes what it thinks ought to be so, " because you have deserved it." But Job knows this is not true. He appeals to Jehovah himself. And he is answered by Jehovah himself. The answer is as simple as that of the three comforters; it is not much more comforting: but it is sublime instead of puerile, it symbolizes a true fact instead of a false hypothesis. The answer is, " Because I am the Lord; because my ways are not your ways; because you cannot understand the divine purpose; because ultimate reality is and always will be a mystery, to be feared as well as loved." [1]

On the other hand, sublime as this idea may be, it still involves all sorts of difficulties on the theistic plane which are avoided if religion does not personify its objects of worship.

  · · · · ·

In this chapter I have attempted to advance two main ideas, both of them unfamiliar. One is that the essence of religion springs from man's capacity for awe and reverence, that the objects of religion, however much rationalized later by intellect or moralized by ethics, however fossilized by convention or degraded by superstition or fear, are in origin and essence those things, events, and ideas which arouse the feeling of sacredness. On this point, with the testimony of anthropologists and archbishops to back me, I hope to have convinced my readers.

The other is that the idea of supernatural divine beings, far from being a necessity to any and every religion, is an intellectual rationalization which was necessary, or at least inevitable, at a certain primitive level of thought and culture; which was then, the crucial assumption once made, worked on by man's intellect and by his ethical sense to give such high conceptions as that of the God of the Jews from after the Exile, or the God of most modern Christian churches; but which now must be abandoned if further religious progress is to be made. Further evidence for these views will be found in subsequent chapters.

[1] Cf. Spinoza's words : " He who truly loves God cannot wish that God should love him in return."

CHAPTER V.

PSYCHOLOGY AND RELIGION

Swiftly I shrivel at the thought of God,
At Nature and its wonders, Time and Space and Death,
But that I, turning, call to thee O soul, thou actual Me,
And lo, thou gently masterest the orbs,
Thou matest time, smilest content at Death,
And fillest, swellest full the vastnesses of space.
Greater than stars or suns,
Bounding O soul thou journeyest forth.
—WALT WHITMAN, *Passage to India.*

We judge the acts of others by our own sympathies, and we judge our own acts by the sympathies of others, every day and all day long, from childhood upwards, until associations, as indissoluble as those of language, are formed between certain acts and the feelings of approbation or disapprobation. It becomes impossible to imagine some acts without disapprobation, or others without approbation of the actor, whether he be one's self or any one else. We come to think in the acquired dialect of morals. An artificial personality, the " man within," as Adam Smith calls conscience, is built up beside the natural personality. He is the watchman of society, charged to restrain the anti-social tendencies of the natural man within the limits required by social welfare.—
T. H. HUXLEY, *Evolution and Ethics.*

(*The Mystic*)

O thou undaunted daughter of desires !
By all thy dower of lights and fires ;
By all the eagle in thee, all the dove ;
By all thy lives and deaths of love ;
By thy large draughts of intellectual day,
And by thy thirsts of love more large than they ;
By all thy brim-filled bowls of fierce desire
By thy last morning's draught of liquid fire. . . .
—R. CRASHAW (on Saint Teresa).

The spirit can for the time pervade and control every member and function of the body, and transmute what in form is the grossest sensuality into purity and devotion.—
THOREAU, *Walden.*

E
55

Nothing but habit could blind us to the strangeness of the fact that the man who believes that morality is based on *a priori* principles, and the man who believes it to be based on the commands of God, the transcendentalist, the theologian, the mystic, and the evolutionist, should be pretty well at one both as to what morality teaches, and as to the sentiments with which its teaching should be regarded.—ARTHUR BALFOUR, *The Foundations of Belief* (1894).

Religion has no doubt already at the savage stage begun to influence moral ideas even in points which have no bearing upon the personal interests of Gods; but this influence is known to have been not nearly so great as it has often been represented, and it seems to me to be a fact not to be doubted that the moral consciousness has originated in emotions entirely different from that feeling of uncanniness and mystery which first led to the belief in supernatural beings.— E. WESTERMARCK, *The Goodness of Gods* (1926).

Men were thought of as free—in order that they might be judged and punished; but consequently every action had to be regarded as voluntary, and the origin of every action had to be imagined as lying in consciousness. In this way the most fundamentally fraudulent characteristic of psychology was established as the very principle of psychology itself.— F. NIETZSCHE, *The Twilight of the Idols*.

THE next point to be discussed concerns the relations of psychology to religion. Here at the outset a warning is needed. It is perfectly clear to those who have eyes to see that the progress of psychology is to-day putting the final storey on the great edifice of naturalism. First the heavenly bodies; then the everyday operations of nature or the earth; then the surface of the earth, its construction and modelling; then the organic kingdoms in their diversity; then the working of the human body and its development; —one after the other came to be comprehensible without reference to supernatural agencies. The human mind and its products have come last. To-day, thanks to men like Stout and James, Shand and McDougall, Charcot and Janet, Freud and Jung —to mention but a few—we are acquiring a knowledge of the laws of the mind and the conditions of its working which are bringing it too into line with the rest. This new knowledge is giving us an entirely new insight into the meaning of the phenomena we have been used to describing under the names of revelation, conversion, grace, salvation, demoniac possession, miracles of healing, prophecy, communion with the divine, and many others. It is showing us that the phenomena thus described, though perfectly definite facts of experience, need not be interpreted in the traditional way. They do not require us to postulate supernatural beings outside ourselves as their cause; they can be accounted for by the natural workings of the individual human mind.

But—and an important but—this need not diminish the value of the phenomena. There exists one class of people who by some strange perversity always maintain that to explain anything is to diminish its intrinsic value. They include the childish minds to whom *omne ignotum pro magnifico* remains a permanent attitude. They also include those who fall into the error of mistaking the parts for the whole, and judging a result by its origins. For everything, no matter how complex, can be analysed into parts; no matter how proud, it has had its humble origin; no matter how vital or how effortless, it must have its underlying machinery. But the parts alone, or their mere sum, are not the whole. The parts, complete to the last bolt, of a motor-car might be presented to the Dalai Lama (or for that matter to me or to you, dear reader!); but they would be very far from being a motor-car, and very little likely to become one without expert help; the parts need arrangement and adjustment before they become a whole.

All this applies with equal truth to the mind. The unitary act of feeling or will is composed of parts in a particular and adjusted relation in precisely the same way that the single act of reaching out the hand and picking up a pencil is compounded out of the balanced actions of a score of separate muscles, guided by a rain of sensory stimuli upon the con-

trolling nerve-centres in the brain. The highest
flower of the spirit is based on lower activities, no
otherwise than a tower upon foundations. The most
powerful minds were once feeble and childish. The
most highly organized scheme of scientific knowledge can be traced back through simpler and less
satisfactory stages to the dimmest and most mistaken
notions; but the value of the knowledge is not
thereby impaired—it remains precisely the same as
it would have been if it had been communicated all
of a piece by a celestial messenger.

Besides this class of mind, whom we may style
the thoughtless analysers, there exists that of the
denigrators or professional blackeners, who, whenever they are confronted with anything unusual,
persist in taking its character away by the simple
expedient of calling it pathological.

But the abnormal is not by any means necessarily
the pathological. The abnormal is that which is not
normal, whether maladjusted or unhealthy, or merely
rare or unusual. Imbecility is abnormal; but so is
genius. Even leaving great genius on one side, if
the average human being (as is not in the least
impossible) were of the mental calibre represented
by a successful barrister, a fine orator, a reasonably
talented man of science or business or affairs, then
what we call a rather backward child, who, to-day,
is unfortunately quite usual and "normal," would
be as abnormal as is a certifiable mental defective in
our present state of civilization. And if we look
back into history, what do we find? That almost
every advance which men have made has been greeted
by no negligible fraction of other men as in some
way abnormal, or worse.

. . . . .

Modern psychology, like so much of science, has
given man reason to feel humbler and less self-
assured than in the "good old days." On the other
hand, again like other scientific advances, it has

shown him how, if he takes its lessons to heart and disciplines his mind in the light of the new knowledge which it has given, he may attain a more limited but more secure confidence, a less ambitious but also less dangerous outlook. It would be presumptuous to attempt a full attack on religious psychology in a single chapter. I shall therefore content myself with a discussion of a few special points of interest, followed by a brief attempt at some general conclusions.

First and foremost come the consequences of evolution and its acceptance. If man's body has evolved, then so has his mind. Our mental powers are not only relative, developed in adaptive relation to the world around us, but there is no reason whatever for supposing them in any way complete. I do not mean theoretically or logically complete—all are agreed upon their incompleteness in this view; but practically, from the standpoint of evolution, there is no inherent reason why the average or the best present human minds should represent the limit of possibility. The mind even of a stupid man can grasp and deal with problems entirely out of the range of a cat's mind; and the problems with which the mind of a great mathematician, or indeed of any genius, deal are at least as high again above those which our stupid friend can tackle. Even if we leave genius on one side, the world would be a very different place if the average inborn ability of men were as high as the average of the most able ten per cent of the population to-day. But there is no reason to leave genius on one side, nor to refuse to face the possibility that mind could be developed by selection to a pitch which would bring its owners to the same height of incomprehensibility to us at our present level of mind, as is our present level to the cats and dogs who sit by the fire and hear us talking, but cannot comprehend.

.   .   .   .   .

A recent much talked-of achievement of psychological science has been the discovery of the subconscious. This has been to psychology what the discovery of the New World was to geography.

The easiest way of understanding what is meant by the subconscious is to take an example from hypnotism. What is called post-hypnotic suggestion is one of the most spectacular and at the same time one of the simplest ways in which the hypnotist can demonstrate the power of suggestion. The operator gives to the subject, during the hypnotic trance, some order which is to be executed only after the lapse of a certain time; he then brings the subject out of the trance, after having also told him not to remember any of the actual events of his trance. At the stated time, the subject will perform the command, but without knowing why he does so. Just before the time for the execution of the command, the subject generally feels uneasy, and will often make up some reason on the spur of the moment for doing what he is really doing under the compulsion of the order of which he has no conscious knowledge. The hypnotizer may, for instance, say to the subject in trance : " In seven minutes' time you will go to the piano, take the silver vase off it, and put it in the centre of the mantelpiece. You will not remember my giving you this order "; and will then wake him. The subject will talk and laugh with the rest; but after five or six minutes will begin to look restlessly about, and then get up and wander across the room, often looking at the vase on the piano. Very possibly he will suddenly say, " I don't like that vase there, do you? I think it would look much better on the mantelpiece "; and with this will take it across to where he has been told, after which his restlessness will leave him.

Such an example demonstrates a number of points. In the first place, the order of which the subject is not conscious has somehow determined his behaviour. Secondly it is much more reasonable to suppose that the order has continued to operate in some mental sphere than to imagine it disappearing wholly from the subject's mind to reappear at the correct moment. We are therefore justified in saying that it was operative in a part of the mind which can best be described as subconscious.[1] In any case, though not itself in consciousness, it influenced the conscious part of the mind.

Thirdly, when the subject gives some reason or excuse for executing the command, he is providing us with an excellent example of rationalization—that is to say, the finding of intellectual reasons for an action which is really being performed under the compulsion of feeling, because we want to or feel we must. Reason is here merely an accessory after the fact; or is reduced to the still more futile office of showing why the stable door should be locked after the horse has been stolen.

In post-hypnotic suggestion the command is in the subconscious and cannot be brought into consciousness. Many other processes, however, may be subconscious, but can be called into consciousness at will. Perhaps the most important of these are habitual acts. When you first begin learning to play the piano, or to use the pen or the typewriter, or to study arithmetic, every step must be, often painfully and toilfully, taken in the full light of consciousness. Practice makes perfect, however; and the chief way in which it makes perfect is by relegating the steps which have been duly learnt to the realm of the unconscious, leaving consciousness free to deal with any new, unlearnt situations that may arise.

Finally, many mental processes may remain in the

[1] Other authors use the term *unconscious*; or *co-conscious*, which can however be applied only to certain cases. See Bernhard Hart, *Lectures on Psychopathology*, 1927, for a discussion of these terms.

unconscious merely for lack of attention. Suppose you are writing with a clock in the room. The ticking of the clock is being registered automatically in your brain, but you are not conscious of it. If some one were to ask you what sounds you could hear, attention would change its focus, and you could at once hear the clock; further, if the clock were suddenly to stop, you would probably be aware of the fact, showing that the ticking noise, though subconsciously, had made part of your general state of mind.

In these two latter cases the subconscious could, by attention or will, be at any moment brought into consciousness. From the biological point of view, we may say that consciousness appears to be needed for dealing with the unforeseen and the complex; accordingly it must not be distracted by being employed upon what is unnecessary or irrelevant to the purpose in hand. A mental organization has been evolved which enables us to focus consciousness by means of attention on one particular activity, other activities being temporarily left in the dim light of the subconscious; it also enables us to relegate what has been thoroughly learned to the unconscious domain, for only so is consciousness left free to build upon what has been learnt, or to learn new types of lessons.

In our first example, however, the subconscious activity could not be brought into consciousness at all : some special machinery prevented the light of attention from reaching it. It is the merit of the last half-century of psychological research to have given us some insight into this process. The French psychologists, with Binet and Janet at their head, introduced the idea of *dissociation* of one part of the mind from the rest. The two both continue to work, but there is no conscious communication between the two. The one part of the consciousness is therefore cut off from the other. This line of work has been especially continued by American psychologists like Morton Prince. Sometimes we find the two dissociated parts of the mind of approximately equal importance; and then usually the two alternate in control of the body, and we have a case of dual personality. But the one may be slightly more important than the other, or a good deal more so, and so on till the state of affairs is reached in which one small tendency or bit of thought-organization is cut off from the main body of the mind's life. Post-hypnotic suggestion represents the extreme in this direction, a single idea being cut off from the rest of the mind for a few minutes.

Meanwhile Freud took the matter a stage further. It may turn out that the majority of Freud's detailed conclusions are false. None the less, as even his opponents agree, he hit upon an idea of the greatest value, which converted the older static psychology of the unconscious into a going concern. He pointed out that painful thoughts and painful events might, through the very intensity of their painfulness, come to be repressed, or banished from consciousness into the unconscious, and held there, like the Titans under Etna, unseen but capable of disturbing the face of the world with their uneasy movements.

In all cases of repression the repressed tendencies, shut out from the light of personal consciousness and from participation, through normal action, in the affairs of the world around, continue to make trouble below the surface. They may influence conscious thoughts; they may dictate courses of action at variance with the ideas of the dominant part of the mind; they and their opponents fight their battles in the darkness of the subconscious, and sap the energy of the soul. When selfish or sensual tendencies are repressed, they may objectify themselves as the prompting of the devil; when it is the altruistic tendencies or the desires for righteousness which are underdog, they may suddenly burst through as the voice of conscience and "make cowards of us all," or be even imagined as the utterances of angels or gods.

To achieve a life approaching the healthy, the two parts of the mental being must come to an understanding. Either the nettle must be gripped, the unpleasant, the terrifying, or the disgusting must be faced, in spite of pain and suffering, and dismissed; or else in some way they must be sublimated, swallowed up in a more exalted and more consuming emotion, as when fear is swallowed up in love of country, the instincts of sex used as the basis for love, the selfish desire for achievement made part of the desire for achievement in unselfish ways, or all three, as in some notable saints, secular as well as religious, merged and utilized in what is usually called loving submission to the will of God.

.   .   .   .   .

Recent psychological work also makes great play with the notion of psychological types. The existence of different types of mind is a fact of observation as old as the hllls : but it is also true that the idea has not been systematically worked out and generalized until very recent years. Jung has been the pioneer in this field. The two extreme types which he distinguishes are the introvert and the extrovert—the mind turned in upon itself, and the mind directed outwards upon the world. The extrovert is interested in things, in immediate experiences of the outside world, in action; the introvert more in his own thought about things, things in their relation to each other and to himself, the bearings of his experiences. The extrovert tends to be social, enjoying the simple expressions of feeling; the introvert has a penchant for solitude, and is concerned with moods and trains of thought more than with direct emotional expression. Thus the introvert tends more to split up his experiencing of the world into neutral outer reality on the one hand, and his own mental life, intellectual and emotional, on the other; while the extrovert tends to keep experience unanalysed, and to leave his thought fused with the outer object which has aroused it.

As McDougall puts it, the extreme extrovert is like a patient under alcohol, he " expresses freely all his emotions, and his affects [states of feeling] pass over immediately into action, each affect in turn finding full expression with but little check from any others." The state of the extreme introvert, on the other hand, is like that of a man under opium : he " dreams rather than acts, and his dreams seem to him more real than the outer world."

Apart from the extreme types and their pathological exaggerations there can be distinguished not only intermediate types, but also, as one would naturally expect, a set of variations on each type. Further, although it is clear that predisposition to one or the other type is largely and usually due to heredity, yet circumstances, too, may have a strong moulding force, and may, for instance, push a man who is of middle type by heredity over from a state of introversion to one of extroversion, or vice versa.

The bearing of these facts on the psychology of religion, however, is what here concerns us.

First and foremost they bid us be tolerant. Men of the two extreme types may get along well enough together, and transact the ordinary affairs of life between themselves; but the one type will never fully comprehend the other. The same object will mean something different to the two. To certain of the extroverted type, especially if they have not received much close intellectual discipline in education, the object is vivid, but remains part of their experience, still clothed with the associated feeling; to an introvert, especially if he has not disciplined himself to overcome his tendencies to shrink into his shell away from hard fact and social contacts, the object is indifferent except as it interests the microcosm of thought or dream which his inner activity is constructing. The extrovert's constant spending of himself in action will seem to the introvert a frittering away of life; while the practical objective extrovert will despise the dreaminess of his counterpart.

In the religious sphere we are familiar with the type of man who is always pursuing, on and on, his thoughts about the universe, about God's nature and his relation to man, about human destiny and salvation; he is the type who constructs the theologies and philosophies which are barely in contact with the solid ground of reality. We are familiar, too, with those whose sole dominant interest is their interior life and the raptures of mystical experience; they construct a whole world of feeling within themselves and are content to leave the world of fact unexplored.

On the other hand we are equally familiar with the hard-headed and energetic religious administrator, who trusts in proper organization of the Church and its activities to achieve the aims of religion, and is concerned not with the niceties of theology but with a clear-cut, accepted creed; with the violent revivalist who pins his faith, without reflection or analysis, to the experiences of the revival meeting, such as sudden conversion, seizures, " speaking with tongues," finds in them objective proof of the existence of the action of a supernatural being, and must be always up and doing in the midst of crowds of people and crowded emotional activity.

The first two types are introverted, the other two extroverted; and one of each type has a predominantly rational or intellectual bias, while the other has a predominantly emotional one.

The religious danger of extreme intellectual introversion is that it leads to hair-splitting dispute, and to the pursuit of theology into regions entirely divorced from reality; extreme emotional introversion, on the other hand, tends to become merely selfish indulgence. Extreme extroversion has its religious dangers too. It belittles thought; it tends to idolatry (in the extended sense of the word) by failing to distinguish properly in religious experience between the object of worship and the feelings which it arouses, with the inevitable result that the feelings, cut off from their true base in the worshipper's mind through his failure to analyse and reflect, become objectified and personified in and behind the object of worship; it tends not only to shallow and noisy revivalism, but also, in other circumstances, to exaggerated ritualism. Remedy in extreme cases there is probably none; but it seems clear that good education (not in the narrow sense of stuffing with facts, but in learning how to use the critical intellect on the one hand, and on the other to have some understanding of the practical handling of objects and of playing a part in social life and organization) is the most valuable corrective against slipping too far in either direction.

The fact that the untrained mind tends to be extroverted is further illustrated by the fact that savages seem to be, on the whole, more extroverted than do civilized. It is clearly of great importance for the history of religion; for it means that the real facts of religious experience will in early religions inevitably tend to find interpretation in a belief that supernatural powers inhere in objects or supernatural beings exist behind them, through the extrovert's failure to disentangle the feeling aroused by an experience from the object which arouses it. In this view, only a raising of the general level of education could bring about any general relinquishing of the belief in personal supernatural beings.

. . . . .

I may now pass to some of the specific psychological experiences of the religious life.

Suggestion is always of great importance; and

correspondingly religious ritual and service is often
so arranged so as to promote suggestibility. The
dim light, the familiar words, the fixed postures,
the isolation from other influences, the general sense
of awe—the whole atmosphere is such as to promote a receptive or suggestible state of mind.
Authority itself helps to suggest the truth of what
it so firmly asserts, and, the receptive state once
induced, the words of the prayers tend to be im-
pressed upon the mind and themselves to exercise
some authority there after the fashion of a suggestion
given in hypnosis. The fact that religious instruction
is usually begun very young, buttresses it with all
kinds of alien strength and makes certain religious
feelings and ideas take root so deeply and so unconsciously that it is extremely hard for the growing mind to break away from them without great
difficulty, and often indeed a profound sense of sin.
This depends partly on the greater suggestibility of
the child, partly on the fact that impressions made
in childhood gather round themselves all sorts of
strong emotional associations.

Suggestibility is also increased by whatever tends
to weaken the natural control of the higher centres
of the brain. Thus, fasting and long vigils will
prepare the mind to receive unquestioningly what
may enter it at such a time.

This brings up a second important set of facts—
namely, those depending on the graded organization
of the mind into what has been called a hierarchy of
different levels, with the degree of dominance of the
higher levels varying from time to time. When the
control exerted by the higher centres is weakened or
removed, the lower centres have free play in ways
which are not possible when they are acting in
subordinate capacities.

The commonest result of the relaxing of the higher
centres' control is for conceptual thought to give
place to imagery, and for the imagery to express the

fulfilment of some normally inhibited desire. The imagery is often distorted, owing to conflict of higher and lower in the mind, so as not to express the desire in too crude and stark a form.

* * *

The same sort of thing, but naturally with many differences, occurs in many so-called mystic experiences—hallucinations of sight or hearing, interior visions or auditions, or ineffable sense of grace or communion. In certain ways it may be said that the mystic experience is on a lower plane than logical thought or moral effort—for it generally substitutes images for concepts, and is also in many cases a wish-fulfilment rather than a wrestling with fact. On the other hand it is only fair to say that the gradual perfection of the mystic experience, which so many of the mystics record, represents a raising of the level in regard to another aspect of mental life—namely, the embracingness of the experience, the comprehension of many aspects of reality, including the highest levels of spiritual perception, in one mental act.

The mystic experience clearly may be of extraordinary beauty and value to those who experience it; and may also be the truest refreshment of the soul wearied with conflict and with work.[1] But with it are involved two dangers—the danger of spiritual selfishness, of prizing the experience at the expense of all else; and the danger of distorted mental development, of forcing the soul into pathological, low-level, or one-sided activities, if the thoughts and desires back of the experience are themselves undisciplined, crude, or feeble.

* * *

The mystics themselves and religious writers in

[1] " What fruit dost thou bring back from this thy vision ? " is the final question which Jacopone da Todi addresses to the mystic's soul. And the answer is : " An ordered life in every state." (Evelyn Underhill, *Mysticism*, p. 23.)

general apply the term *prayer* to all kinds of experiences to which its ordinary use in the sense of petition could not be applied. This brings us to some consideration of ordinary or petitionary prayer such as is prescribed in the Book of Common Prayer and is habitual, morning and evening, with most Christians. On reflection it will be seen to have two functions; one which has meaning only if the worshipper has a real belief in a personal deity who can influence the course of events; and another which has meaning only in so far as the worshipper has a real desire for his own spiritual alteration, or for experience of those attributes which he associates with this deity, attributes of sanctity and awfulness, of power and tremendous mystery, of goodness and love, of beauty and wisdom. These two motives are inextricably mixed in the prayers of Christian churches and indeed of most theistic religions.

Without some of the second element, prayer is in itself valueless as a spiritual exercise, and tends, by a natural psychological process, to degenerate. For if prayer is a mere petition, nothing should matter so long as it is in due form, and reaches its destination. All the other functions of prayer, however, are in reality functions of contemplation and meditation rather than petition. The contemplation may be of some intense desire of the worshippers, such as the desire for purity, and so be cast in the form of a petition; but the psychological machinery will not operate unless the idea permeates the mind. Prayer of this contemplative type is one of the central kernels of developed religion. It permits the bringing before the mind of a world of thought which in most people must inevitably be absent during the occupations of ordinary life : it allows the deepest longings of the soul, driven down below the surface by circumstance, to come into action : and it is the means by which the mind may fix itself upon this or that noble or beautiful or awe-inspiring idea, and so grow to it and come to realize it more fully.

. . . . .

One other very frequent psychological element in religion is what may be called the desire to escape from self. The psychological basis of this would seem to be fairly easy to comprehend, although details will obviously differ at different levels of culture. On the one hand the feeling of the self or ego builds itself up gradually out of the chaotic mind-life of the infant; and in the process some activities and thoughts are closely woven together into the texture of the "I," others remain outside or are repressed or but loosely connected, and when they irrupt and make connection with the ego, they are frequently felt as "not-I," and therefore belonging to some external power or being.

The other root of the desire to escape from self is the desire to be rid of the burden of sin. I have not the space to embark on this formidable topic. But I can perhaps throw out a few hints towards its better consideration. Two important facts meet us at the outset—namely, that the sense of sin is often much more strongly developed in what the opinion of the world would class as quite virtuous people than in genuine criminals. Indeed, modern psychological study makes it clear that a considerable proportion of criminals become criminal because they are endowed by heredity with a subnormal moral sense, an insufficient capacity for experiencing the sense of sin at all. In the second place, we often find that the sense of sin may be strongly aroused by infringing apparently neutral, stupid, or meaningless injunctions, much less so by the transgression of universally-recognized moral rules.

The first fact depends upon the psychological truism, that there cannot be a sense of sin without a conflict. In general, the stronger the conflict, the stronger the sense of sin. This is well illustrated by the records

F

of those who have experienced sudden conversion; they almost invariably exaggerate, often to a ludicrous extent, the sinfulness of perfectly ordinary worldly activities, or of trivial moral lapses which occurred before their conversion. The second fact depends upon the power of taboos to acquire a formidable charge of sanctity.

The doctrine of original sin is a theological perversion of natural fact. It is a fact that all human beings begin life with an equipment of instincts, impulses, and desires, at war with one another and often out of harmony with the realities of the physical, social, and spiritual world. A child is like an animal or a bird in that one impulse at a time comes into full possession of its mental life, only to be replaced by another in a flash when the time comes. Rational self-restraint, altruism, and control, the uniting of the separate impulses into a unitary mental organism, and the moulding of this in adaptation to reality, can only come with the growth of reasoned reflection and emotional illumination.

Sin and the sense of sin will always be with us, to torture and weigh down; but it is safe to prophesy that the religion of the future will try to prevent men being afflicted with the sense of sin, rather than first encouraging it and then curing it.

．　　　．　　　．　　　．

So far I have said little about what is often spoken of as the kernel of religion—namely, faith. This has been because faith can hardly be considered without some study of its psychological basis. As a start I may quote from Thouless, who writes on religious psychology from the standpoint of a psychologist who is also a professing Christian. " The method by which our beliefs are influenced by other people is not, on the whole, reasoned demonstration. The child does not have the existence of God proved to it in its religious lessons. It is still true in later life that the simple affirmation of religious doctrines by a person for whom we have respect, or the mere fact of the holding of such doctrines by the persons amongst whom we live, may have an authority over us compared with which the influence of the most convincing chain of reasoning is negligible. The method by which beliefs are transmitted to us otherwise than by reasoned demonstration is *suggestion*."

Professor McDougall, discussing the matter on purely scientific grounds, writes that suggestion is " the imparting of a proposition in such a manner that it is accepted with conviction, independently of any logical grounds for such conviction."

Further, all authors are agreed that suggestion in the ordinary waking state differs only from suggestion in hypnotic trance in that the effects observed are not so extreme.

The precise methods by which suggestion is brought about need not concern us deeply. In all cases, however, there comes in the feature that an idea obtains authority over our mind, and becomes accepted with a powerful sense of conviction, quite apart from its appeal to reason, logic, or experience. In a good case of hypnotism the dissociation is practically complete. In ordinary suggestion, where the individual in his waking state accepts statements made by some authority without bothering about their logical implications, the dissociation is only partial.

In most cases of waking suggestion, however, the fact suggested is either not too unlike ordinary experience to be impossible; or it has a basis of real truth; or the logical and rational reasons against its truth are unfamiliar or difficult of comprehension. The success of the confidence trick depends on the actuality of real confidence between friends; the belief of the Christian Scientist reposes upon the real fact that much pain can be made to disappear by not brooding over it; the suggestion that a particular garb or lack of garb is indecent depends upon the fact that indecency exists; the belief in witchcraft or in a flat or a central earth is possible because the chain of reasoning which excludes magic or demands a spherical circling globe is comparatively complex.

It might be thought, if suggestion always depended upon a partial disregard of our mental watch-dog, rational experience, that it must always be undesirable, and that it was very difficult to understand its origin on evolutionary principles. On the contrary, suggestibility can, on a little reflection, be seen to be a biological necessity, particularly in the early stages of man's evolution. If it is necessary for certain types of action to be performed in strict accord with the dictates of reason and experience, it is equally necessary for other actions to be performed unquestioningly at the behest of authority or of communal feeling. We all know that only one man can be captain aboard ship; and that what counts in war is victory.

But, even apart from emergencies like war, suggestibility and suggestion are necessary for any community. To take the scientific sphere alone, it is probably quite impossible to-day for any one man, however brilliant and hard-working, to master the main evidence in all fields of scientific knowledge. How much more impossible, then, for the man with limited leisure to do so. This means, however, that many of the ideas of science must either be taken on trust by a great number of people, or else not accepted at all. In education, even the most ardent advocates of the child's finding things out for himself admit that, life being short and knowledge infinite, it is impossible to apply the principle radically, but that the child must be told some things and must believe them.

We may sum up by saying that not only the concerted relation of leadership and subordination would be impossible without some suggestibility, but also the diffusion of knowledge.

On the other hand—and this is a vital point— suggestibility need not be abject, nor faith blind or misdirected. The educated man need not be able to follow all the evidence on which the modern theory of the atom or the hereditary constitution is based; but he can have a basis of scientific training and knowledge and an understanding of scientific method which makes his acceptance a reasonable one. The sailor need not understand the reasons for the order given by his superior officer; but he can understand why obedience on shipboard is necessary, and not merely obey like a dog.

We may put it from a slightly different angle. Suggestibility and its results, obedience and faith irrespective of logical reasoning, are characters of the human species, mental properties which exist whether we like them or not; and they can be employed, like any other of the raw materials of the human mind, either well or ill.

Once it is properly appreciated that faith rests upon precisely the same basis as hypnotic suggestion, religiously-minded people should be the first to see that the faith which they have should not be purely arbitrary, the result of authority alone, but rational. Is not faith the sum of our beliefs as they predispose us to thought and action, whether these beliefs are purely reasoned, or purely suggested, or based on suggestion tempered with reason; and ought it not to be a reproach instead of a boast that faith can be upheld in opposition to reason, and human nature, here again, divided against itself?

.   .   .   .   .

Ritual also deserves some consideration. This does not, so much as theology, become attached secondarily to the religious emotion, but rather grows directly out of it as its immediate expression. In some cases, even, non-moral actions (such as those performed in a state of exaltation) may be regarded as in themselves sacred, and here ritual, in the form of these actions, may make a primary contribution to the sum of religion.

On the other hand, so soon as intellect and morality

have been roped in to become part of the field of religion, conclusions can be drawn from them which demand fulfilment in ritual.

The simplest forms of ritual are those actions which are the natural accompaniments of a sense of awe or reverence : obeisance, kneeling, or prostration; exclamations; great care for the object of reverence, and a desire to adorn and beautify it. But there are certain actions and their accompanying feelings which are almost universally regarded as sacred by primitive man owing to the sense which accompanies them of being possessed by some fresh and external power—the various states of exaltation.

Exaltation may come in connection with epileptic fits; with intoxication; with the taking of various drugs; with dancing; with the communal frenzies, recorded even at many modern revivals, of " shaking " and of " speaking with tongues." In so far as the sense of exaltation can be obtained at all by deliberate performance of certain actions, the ritual of these actions may be embodied as an integral part of a religion.

Eskimo and Indian priests (medicine-men) are often chosen on account of epileptic tendencies : certain Dervishes produce a state of religious exaltation by violent dancing, as do various negro tribes; Rivers records how among the Todas of India divination may be accompanied by a species of hysterical " possession "; the automatism known as " speaking with tongues," or in later psychological parlance as *glossolalia*, was highly prized by the early Christians as part of their religious life; the Bacchanals combined wine and the dance to produce a mystic frenzy; the modern sect of Shakers live up to their name; and extraordinary scenes of the sort are recorded of revivalist camp-meetings in America.

In such cases the ritual imposes itself directly as a part of the religious life. But when, for instance, belief in a powerful supernatural being prompts the adoption of rites of propitiation by sacrifice or offering, the ritual is added consequentially.

The highest forms of ritual are those in which the two aspects are united; ritual at its best is like a good work of art in that it both expresses and generates emotion and thought.

The difficulties which have grown up concerning ritual in the last few centuries are on the whole secondary difficulties, the necessary consequence of primary difficulties in the sphere of theology. Many of the Puritan and Protestant difficulties (like the difficulties of the great controversy about image-worship in the eighth century) about " idols," visible images and pictures, the virtual worship of saints, and so forth, have a theological origin. If God is essentially a *purely* spiritual being, then it is logical to worship him by the aid of pure spirit alone, and any material representation is a degradation of this spirituality. But common sense has usually triumphed over this logical point, and allowed a reasonable symbolism.

.   .   .   .   .

Another important point may perhaps be considered here : I am thinking of the satisfaction of religious feeling in ways which are outside the domain of religion as ordinarily understood and as organized in a Church. Do not let us forget that in the Middle Ages the Church extended its sway over many more departments of life than it does to-day. The church building had not yet been cut off by the puritan spirit as a bare House of God to the exclusion of all else. As a place for the exhibition of sacred and natural rarities, it served as a museum : it was usually the nearest thing to an art-gallery : as stage for the mystery plays it was a theatre, as place of plainsong and chanted mass a concert-room : the reading of the Bible stories in the lessons was half the average man's chance of literature.

The church porch is still used for many official notices : in old days it was much more both of a social and a business centre. In addition, before the rise of the universities, monasteries were among the chief centres of scholarship and of medical knowledge as well as of various arts and crafts. That is all gone. There is now a division of function, and we have our museums, our art-galleries, our concert-halls, libraries, theatres, our secular universities; and the functions of the church, both as organization and as edifice, are narrowed down.

From the point of view of the diffusion of thought and ideas man has passed through four main stages and is now entering upon a fifth. He began with speech alone. He proceeded to the invention of writing, and so to the greater permanence and accuracy of his tradition. Then came printing, with the possibility of multiplication of the written word. With the industrial era there came the substitution of machine-power for man-power, with a consequent new multiplication of the multiplying capacity of the printing-press, and therefore the possibility of the dissemination of ideas literally to everybody, in every place, owing to the cheapness of mass-production.

Finally, in the last half-century or so, we have entered upon a new era, whose implications and whose possibilities we have hardly yet envisaged. This is the era of new modes of spreading human thought and human achievement. Even if we leave out photography and telegraphy, there remain the invention of the gramophone, the invention of the cinema, the discovery of wireless, and the perfection of cheap colour-printing. All these, in their several ways, are completely altering the whole problem of the diffusion of culture, and so of the growth of culture and civilization itself. Not only is the spread of ideas and knowledge, already facilitated by writing and printing, now again facilitated and speeded up, but the achievements of the human spirit in music and painting can to-day be spread and enjoyed in ways previously impossible.

What, it may perhaps be asked, has this to do with religion? It has a good deal to do with it. Before the perfection of writing, religion could not but be mainly a social affair; its social ceremonials and professed belief were the chief way of expression for the religious spirit. With the introduction of writing it was possible for those who could read and write to find an outlet in writing for the expression of their own personal ideas, and, in reading, to commune with the thoughts of other individuals, in addition to participating in the un-individual, socialized thought and feeling of organized religion. This process was accelerated by the introduction of printing, but so long as books were dear and education restricted— that is to say, even in the most civilized countries, until the middle of last century—organized religion was bound to remain socialized if it was to affect the bulk of the community.

But now industrialism, universal education, improved transport and communications, and the progress of invention are putting a different complexion on affairs. You remember what Milton once wrote: "A good book is the precious life-blood of a master spirit, embalmed and treasured up on purpose to a life beyond life." If the spiritual life-blood of the great masters of thought is available to everyone, why go to church and listen to familiar prayers and to a prosy sermon, when you could stay at home and receive new knowledge and deeper thoughts from a book? Goethe, Emerson, Wordsworth, Blake, Carlyle, Dante, Sir Thomas Browne, Shelley, and the rest of the assembly of immortal spirits—they jostle each other on your shelves, each waiting only to be picked up to introduce you to his own unique and intense experience of reality.

The Origin of Species is to-day a good deal more profitable as theology than the first chapter of Genesis, and William James's *Principles of Psychology* will be a better commentary on the Decalogue than any hortatory sermon. The poetry of Herbert or Donne or Vaughan, of Francis Thompson or Walt Whitman, will introduce you to new ways of mystic feeling; Trevelyan's *History of England* is likely to be a more salutary history lesson, because nearer home, than the historical books of the Old Testament; Whitehead's *Science and the Modern World* is more likely to help the perplexed mind of a twentieth-century Englishman than the apocalyptic visions of Revelation or the neo-Platonic philosophy of the Fourth Gospel; to sacrifice a score of Sundays to making acquaintance with the ideas of other great religions like Buddhism would be very much preferable, even from the purely religious point of view, to continuance in the familiar round and the familiar narrowness of one's own church.

What is more, there is no reason whatever why in all such activity you should not in your degree be participating in the religious life. All philosophy and science, all great art, all history, all lives of men—one and all may inspire to reverence or exaltation, or be made the subject of reflection which, being concerned with great problems in a grave and reverent way, is more truly religious than any pietism.

It might be said that if this is the case, there is no room left for organized worship. I do not think this is so. There will always remain the religious satisfaction of plunging the mind in a common, social act, and always a satisfaction in familiar ritual hallowed by time and association. There is also to many people a satisfaction in symbolism; and to others in finding, in the combined privacy and publicity of the church service, a simultaneous release from the world and from the individual self.

On the other hand, it seems clear that the more opportunities there are for satisfying this or that aspect of the religious life outside a set service and a church building, the less important will service and building become.

CHAPTER VI

DEVELOPED RELIGION

The consciousness that something in life is sacred, worth living and dying for, is one of humanity's moral indispensables, and religion is the fruitful mother of it.—Rev. H. E. FOSDICK.

It is very strange; want itself is a treasure in Heaven; and so great a one that without it there could be no treasure. . . . You must want like a God that you may be satisfied like a God.

Love is deeper than at first it can be thought. It never ceases but in endless things.—THOMAS TRAHERNE, *Centuries of Meditations*.

The decay of Christianity and Buddhism, as determinative influences in modern thought, is partly due to the fact that each religion has unduly sheltered itself from the other. The self-sufficient pedantry of learning and the confidence of ignorant zealots have combined to shut up each religion in its own forms of thought. Instead of looking to each other for deeper meanings, they have remained self-satisfied and unfertilised.

Both have suffered from the rise of the third tradition, which is science, because neither of them had retained the requisite flexibility of adaptation. Thus the real, practical problems of religion have never been adequately studied in the only way in which such problems *can* be studied, namely, in the school of experience.—A. N. WHITEHEAD, *Religion in the Making* (1927).

As I stood behind the coffin of my little son the other day, with my mind bent on anything but disputation, the officiating minister read, as a part of his duty, the words, " If the dead rise not again, let us eat and drink, for to-morrow we die." I cannot tell you how inexpressibly they shocked me. Paul had neither wife nor child, or he must have known that his alternative involved a blasphemy against all that was best and noblest in human nature. I could have laughed with scorn. What! because I am face to face with irreparable loss, . . . I am to renounce my manhood, and, howling, grovel in bestiality. Why, the very apes know better, and if you shoot their young the poor brutes grieve

81

their grief out and do not immediately seek distraction in a
gorge.—T. H. HUXLEY, *Life and Letters*.

I cannot but say that I believe that some day our conception of God will have become independent of nearly all that
has come into it from the primitive Jewish tribal and other
pagan conceptions of God which have passed into Christianity,
and that our conception will be constantly renewed and
growing from all human knowledge and experience, from all
science, philosophy, and psychology.—Canon J. M. WILSON,
in *The Modern Churchman* (1924).

> Serene will be our days and bright,
> And happy will our nature be,
> When Love is an unerring light,
> And Joy its own security.
> —WILLIAM WORDSWORTH, *Ode to Duty*.

THE future remains. What is it to bring forth?
Religion, if it is to be vital not only to the individual
but also to the community, makes three demands.
It must be a deeply-felt personal way of life—a way
of life based on a particular emotional and spiritual
approach, certain beliefs, and certain preferences in
the realm of values.

In so far as definite religious communities or
churches exist, these must have some sort of organization of their own.

But finally—and this has been much lost sight of
in the past, owing to the unfortunate dualism underlying most religious thought and popular philosophy
—the religious communities and the lives of individual religious people must have some organic
relation with the community as a whole, their thought
with its thought, their morals with its morals, their
feelings with its feelings. We are apt to forget that
the world is really growing up. How can the twen-
tieth century, which is not only actually but inevitably
new, be content with the same religious outlook
which satisfied it when the natural world was uncom-
prehended and appeared chaotic as much as orderly,
and the ideas of control and conscious change had
not yet been born? We may feel it natural and even

desirable that a religion such as Christianity, for instance, should at its origin have set itself up as definitely hostile to the whole outlook of the world into which it was born; that when science was almost non-existent, morals chaotic, cruelty rampant, force the one great arbiter, and religions of every complexion, including those of barbaric crudity and beastliness, were jostling each other, all tolerated, in the imperial city, Christianity should have proclaimed itself not merely as a way of salvation, but as the only way.

But to-day humanity is facing the possibility of attaining its maturity. We cannot really think it tolerable that it should be faced with perpetual conflict at the central heart of its being. If its maturity is to be stable or fully fruitful, it will be necessary for any religion of the future to be an aspect of its unitary and interconnected thought and life, not one of two opposing tendencies.

I feel that any such religion of the future must have as its basis the consciousness of sanctity in existence—in common things, in events of human life, in the gradually-comprehended interlocking whole revealed to human desire for knowledge, in the benedictions of beauty and love, in the catharsis, the sacred purging, of the moral drama in which character is pitted against fate and even deepest tragedy may uplift the mind.

What we live by must be organized : the different ideas and aspirations, the goals and springs of conduct, must be brought into relation with each other and with a full experience of outer reality, in the widest possible way. This is where *organized* religious thought makes its contribution to civilization.

In any such intellectual organization of religious thought there appear to me to be three main categories to be considered. The first is constituted by the powers of nature; the second by the ideal goals of the human mind; the third by actual living beings, human and other, in so far as they embody such ideals.

As we have already seen, the personification and glorification of these would give us an approximation to the theological doctrine of the Trinity, though in various details, especially as regards the first person, there would still remain considerable differences.

Mr. H. G. Wells proposed the name " The Veiled Being " for a conception closely akin to my first one. I find the term misleading. In so far as the reality herein included is in truth a spiritual Being, it is so completely Veiled as to recede into the unapproachable realms where, for instance, dwells Herbert Spencer's " Unknowable." And in so far as the reality is not veiled, it is definitely not a Being. If a name is required, *power*, it seems to me, should be the noun. What is apprehended by the religious consciousness here is the Eternal Power which is outside man, power possibly in part spiritual, certainly in all its most obvious aspects material.

Corresponding to the third person of the Trinity (and in this scheme, too, logically coming last) is Pure Spirit or Idea. It is constituted by the sum of man's general and ultimate notions about truth, beauty, goodness. It forms a definite and real part of the atmosphere in which human beings grow up. Since it consists of general ideas, its implications can never be exhausted, it always urges man on to goals which can never be completely attained. It is, indeed, spirit in its most religious form, and in so far as a natural object for religious feeling, a Holy Spirit, even if completely impersonal.

The third may perhaps be best thought of, from the point of view of religion, as spirit realizing itself in living matter—spirit progressively embodied, eventually coming to exert a control over nature and life. At its lowest it is a spark of spirit dimly and unconsciously sharing existence with material body; at its highest it is conscious spirit directing evolution in accordance with its desires and will; throughout, it is a movement towards more mind, expressing itself in the realities of individual lives, characters, and achievements. It connects the other two aspects of reality. It is Incarnate Spirit, embodied in Life the Mediator.

These ideas can, of course, be analysed and dissected. It is the function of science to do so in the most detailed and dispassionate way possible; of philosophy to relate them to its metaphysical background; of theology to discuss them in relation to man and his personal and racial destinies. Enough, however, will have been said to show that this analysis can be properly made; meanwhile the idea of natural fact and power remains something nitary, a perfectly genuine conception, however detailed an analysis physics, chemistry, and the rest of the natural sciences may make of its component parts : and the same is true of the psychological analysis of the second and the biological analysis of the third idea.

These three categories of fact are, however, closely related. Abstract ideas and pure ideals are properties of living human organisms; human organisms are continuously linked with all other organisms, plant and animal, by the evolutionary process; and this existing stream of organic life must itself have evolved continuously from non-living matter.

All three are merely different aspects of one reality; and, in so far as our human destiny is concerned, the historical processes at work have been such as to make the spiritual or mental sides of this one reality emerge from insignificance into greater and greater importance until they come largely to dominate and control the material aspects.[1]

A recognition of these relationships and this unity

[1] Malthus was expressing the same general idea in terms of a different system of thought when, in his celebrated Essay (1st ed., p. 294), he wrote : " The impressions and excitements of this world are the instruments with which the Supreme Being forms matter into mind."

is equally essential with the recognition of the three separate sets of facts.

Thomas Hardy, throughout his writings, stressed the arbitrary and capricious power, indifferent to human life and human thought, as which it seems to me External Nature must be perceived by any one not blinded by theological preconceptions or his own desires. Where I would suggest he went astray was in setting this up as the essential reality, and in neglecting to notice its relationship to the other realities I have been discussing.

The three categories themselves, and their relationship, are not the same thing as the sum of the isolated brute facts which go to compose them. They are the facts as apprehended by the powers of the mind—they are reality embodied in experience, and so becoming organized and unified into an ordered and more vital reality.

Had the word God not come, almost universally, to have the connotation of supernatural personality, it could be properly employed to denote this unity. For if my reasoning has been correct, what has been called God by men has been precisely this reality, or various aspects of it, but obscured by symbolic vestures. Perhaps the day will come when men will recognize this, and throw away the veils. Until that time, it is best to use some other word or phrase. In any case this reality, as a proper object for the religious sentiment, is something unitary and deserves a name. For the moment I shall call it the Sacred Reality. The precise term, however, does not matter. What does matter is the recognition that the experience of the universe as affecting human life and therefore as invested with sanctity is a reality, and is the proper object of religion.[1]

[1] Cf. George Santayana (Introduction to *The Ethics of Spinoza*): "The spirit of God, accordingly, means simply the genius of men, the ground of which lies indeed beyond them, in the universal context and influence of nature; but the conscious expression and fruition of it first arises in them severally, as occasion warrants"

As regards the relationship of this reality to human life one further comment is in place. The category of Natural Power transcends human life on the material side, as matter. It is external, and what is given in it is alien and unfamiliar. Humanity is one combination of the elements of reality; but there are an infinity of others, some exceedingly diverse. Humanity, however, consists of a number of bits of living matter, and is thus rooted in what transcends it.

The category of pure spirit also transcends humanity, but on the spiritual side, and in a different way. It transcends any and every particular by being general, exceeds anything and everything actual by being ideal, and yet the capacity for thinking in these general and ideal terms is a capacity of particular and actual human beings. Humanity is much more intimately entangled with this aspect of reality, and transcendence and immanence are there more intricately interwoven.

When we come down to more detail, there are many facts which need to be taken into account to get a proper picture of reality. We must accept, for instance, the fact that men are not fundamentally equal, but unequal in being endowed by the natural processes of reproduction with chemically different outfits of hereditary units. Development, both of body and mind, achievements and character, is a gradual realization of some of the potentialities inherent in these outfits. Development is a true *epigenesis*, to use the technical term, a bringing into existence of actually new and more complex organization. It is brought about by interaction of the hereditary outfit with the outer environment. Factors in hereditary constitution or in environment may very definitely limit the possibilities of development both on the physical and the mental side. If, for instance, one particular human hereditary unit be different from normal in a particular way, the human organism is incapable, always and inevitably, of

G

distinguishing the colours red and green : or, if one particular chemical substance be absent from the child's diet, it will inevitably grow up stunted and deformed, a sufferer from rickets.

Though the conditions in respect of higher intellectual and spiritual characters are clearly much more complex, the same undoubtedly holds good for them as well. The automatic working of Mendelian law may, to take an extreme example, produce a congenital imbecile, who is no more capable of any comprehension of what a Christian means by God than he is of lecturing on advanced physics ; and the converse is seen in those whose hereditary outfit equips them from the start with more than usual talent, in music, say, or mathematics, or spiritual sensitiveness. But, *per contra*, those same talents can unfold into actuality only when they develop in a suitable environment ; a wolf-child could not become a mathematician, nor could a paleolithic man, in the absence of musical tradition and musical instruments, have become a great musician.

Destiny is the limiting force of heredity and environment ; and freedom is human plasticity—the immense variety of possible development opening before a man endowed with a definite heredity.

At first sight this may seem to throw light on the eternal conflict between predestination and free-will. In part, perhaps, it does so ; but on such a view the free-will would only be apparent. What at any rate is certain is that the sense of free-will, with the accompanying fact of envisaging alternatives between which to choose, is essential for action at high levels. Many of the leaders of religious thought have stressed the fact that the choice of the right alternative is inevitable to a mind which has both truly seen and truly felt the meaning of two alternatives. The intellectual parallel is instructive. What is essential and what is difficult in an intellectual problem is to see the intellectual alternatives clearly and to amass sufficient knowledge concerning their implications. Once this is done the solution is inevitable.

I have previously urged the view that mind and matter are merely two inseparable aspects of one more fundamental substance. Along somewhat similar lines it may be said that what we call the sense of effort is, at one time or another, necessary in the process of achievement, and that the simultaneous holding of alternatives in the mind, with consequent sense of indetermination and need for choice, is a necessity for moral and spiritual as for intellectual advance. Certain it is that the freedom of the will is in a way paradoxical; for the more disciplined and efficient the mind and the more clearly and fully the alternatives are envisaged, the quicker and more effortless is the choice—and yet the greater is the sense of freedom and spontaneity in the choice. It may well be that the controversy will turn out to be an unreal one, based on a false logic in the definition of freedom; and that what we call freedom consists essentially in the power of envisaging a number of alternatives together in the mind, while mere arbitrariness and non-determinate choosing, which is often thought to be the essence of free-will, is really something which cannot exist and can indeed not really be *thought* at all.[1]

One salient way in which man differs from other animals is in the much greater range of potentiality given to him. There is very little difference between two healthy jelly-fish; a little more, but still not

[1] Cf. Professor Munsterberg (*Psychology and Physiology*, p. 7): "Freedom of will means absence of an outer force or of pathological disturbance in the causation of our actions. We are free, as our actions are not the mere outcome of conditions which lie outside of our organism, but the product of our own motives and their normal connections. All our experiences and thoughts, our inherited disposition and trained habits, our hopes and fears, co-operate in our consciousness and in its physiological substratum, the brain, to bring about the action."

much, between two monkeys; but the difference between two normal men may easily exceed the difference between a jelly-fish and a monkey. This difference is, of course, mainly in the mind; but the mind is the most important part of man.

From another aspect it is equally clear that, had circumstances been but a little different, a human mind might have developed into a mental organism quite different from its actual state; and equally that even the best-developed minds fail to realize more than a fraction of the possibilities open to them, and that the average man allows his mind to remain a baby instead of encouraging it to grow up, lives all his life like a chrysalis in a cocoon without realizing that he might, if he wished, emerge winged.

Out of this raw material of possibilities man builds his personality. Sometimes he does not realize what lies waiting to his hand; at others he concentrates on some parts only of the mental dispositions, and (consciously or more often unconsciously) represses the rest. These neglected or repressed realities of being have a way of taking their revenge and suddenly flooding up into consciousness, so that the personality which had thought itself secure, in the privacy of its smug self-imposed limitations, suddenly finds itself in the presence of tremendous forces, not personal, and yet part of its own flesh and blood, vital realities which it had thought to escape, now confronting it and threatening, unless both welcomed and disciplined, to strike it down from off its pedestal of equilibrium.

One of the most insidious enemies of true freedom is this unreasoned repression of certain instincts and all things connected with them. They continue to work in the subterranean part of the mind, and to influence the process of thought going on above, so that consciousness is all the time finding reasons for acting in this or that way, rather than using reason.

Thus a false organization of the self, with its failure to unify the raw materials of spiritual gifts and its unresolved conflicts of desires or values, is a powerful source of instability and incompleteness, and must distort or cramp the religious outlook. On the other hand, the most potent force for ensuring that the personality shall be stably organized is a proper scale of values.

Primitive man receives most of his scale of values ready-made; he imbibes them like the air he breathes; they are hard set in the tribal customs and standards whose foundations he does not even think about, much less question. The educated modern, however, must contribute something of his own effort to his scale of values. If he be not a spiritual and intellectual cipher, he will, however much he may have unconsciously absorbed during childhood, be faced with the need for readjusting his ideas as experience is forced upon him. Once he is compelled to look into the matter, he will find that vast stores of experience, gathered by others, are available to him in books and in the minds of living men, and he is driven on, if he is worth his salt, until he has explored the main lines of knowledge, however cursorily, for himself, and found out what kinds of fact there are which bear upon his personal problems.

Developed religion from this point of view may be thought of as confronting the external world with an inner scale of values, and attempting to harmonize the two in life. If to this it be added that the specifically religious feeling of sacredness and reverence must play its part in the ceaseless encounter between outer and inner, the result is a good working definition. It may also be added that, from the standpoint of the individual, development and change must enter into the process. The child's mind cannot but be unorganized, must lack experience, must work on the childish plane, with crude association instead of sharpened reason, with undisciplined wish and phantasy instead of tempered desire and purpose. The passage from a childish to a mature way of thinking and feeling, from the infantile to the adult mental plane, is necessary. In the process experience alters the scale of values, and they in their turn alter the way of dealing with experience.

The various ways in which the individual spirit may succeed or fail, partly or wholly, in this traject from infancy to true manhood, are the province of the psychologist. It may, however, be safely asserted that for the majority of human beings, though by no means all, a scale of values which includes elements of a religious nature is needed if the development is to be at all complete or satisfactory.

I would accordingly like to supplement my more comprehensive but static definitions, which I intended to apply to primitive as well as to developed religion, by something more specifically the concern of modern civilization, applying only to developed religion in which general ideas of morality and reason have asserted their right to attach themselves to the primitive concept of sacredness and to modify and extend the domain of religion and its expression.

A developed religion, then, must satisfy the following requirements. It will not merely be confined to man's more or less immediate reaction to the mysterious or sacred; it will not be content with a system (often incomplete or self-contradictory) of mythology or of primitive rationalization as its theology; nor only with traditional ritual or formalism as its code of action. On the contrary it will always extend its conception of what is sacred and a proper object of religious feeling to include man's destiny and his relation with the rest of the world; it will apply the pure force of intellect to its ideas, and attempt a theology or intellectual basis which shall be both logical and comprehensive, accurate and coherent; it will also inevitably perceive that ethics and morality are keystones of human destiny, and link up its sacred beliefs with a pure ethic and a reasoned morality. It will, in a word, not be content to leave its religious life chaotic and unordered, with loose ends unconnected with the rest of reality, but will come more and more consciously to aim at an organized and unified scheme of religion, which further shall be connected with all other parts of the mental life; and it will attempt to achieve this by putting forward a scheme of belief and a scale of values around and over which man's aspirations to sacredness in emotion, thought, and action may most securely grow.

Thus a developed religion should definitely be a relation of the personality as a whole to the rest of the universe, one into which reverence enters, and one in which the search for the ultimate satisfactions of discovering and knowing truth, experiencing and expressing beauty, and ensuing the good in righteous action, all have the freest possible play.

Any conflict which prevents the personality from attaining wholeness is a hindrance : all taboos against considering any part of the universe in relation to man and his destiny are hindrances : so, too, are all restrictions upon the free use of reason, or the free appeal to conscience.

An undeveloped religion does impede human faculty.

A developed religion is one which is so organized that it helps to unify the diverse human faculties, and to give each of them the fullest play in a common task.

CHAPTER VII

CONCLUSION

All parts away for the progress of souls;
All religion, all solid things, arts, governments—all that was
    or is apparent upon this globe or any globe, falls into
    niches and corners before the procession of souls along the
    grand roads of the universe.
Of the progress of the souls of men and women along the
    grand roads of the universe, all other progress is the
    needed emblem and sustenance.—WALT WHITMAN, *The
    Song of the Open Road.*

I that saw where ye trod
    The dim paths of the night,
Set the shadow called God
    In your skies to give light;
But the morning of manhood is risen, and the
        shadowless soul is in sight.

The tree many-rooted
    That swells to the sky,
With frondage red-fruited
    The life-tree am I;
In the buds of your lives is the sap of my leaves; ye
    shall live and not die.

But the Gods of your fashion
    That take and that give,
In their pity and passion
    That scourge and forgive,
They are worms that are bred in the bark that falls off;
    they shall die and not live.
        —ALGERNON CHARLES SWINBURNE, *Hertha.*

To see a World in a grain of sand,
    And a Heaven in a wild flower,
Hold Infinity in the palm of your hand,
    And Eternity in an hour.
        —WILLIAM BLAKE, *Auguries of Innocence.*

Through love, through hope, through faith's transcendent
    dower,
We feel that we are greater than we know.
        —WILLIAM WORDSWORTH, *The River Duddon.*

Your creeds are dead, your rites are dead,
   Your social order too.
Where tarries he, the Power who said:
   See, I make all things new.
         —MATTHEW ARNOLD, *Obermann.*

THE critic of what is established, the opponent of orthodoxy, whether the orthodoxy be theological or economic, is almost invariably reproached for his destructiveness. It is true that there is such a thing as mere iconoclasm, and that certain types of minds are so powerfully moved by love of truth that the least inaccuracy or logical flaw is abhorrent to them, or find certain aspects of popular religion so grotesque or so abhorrent that religion as a whole seems tarred with the same brush. To them, religion is something to be attacked. They never pause to ask whether it be a good thing to throw out the baby with the bath : indeed, it is probable that most of them have not noticed the baby, and would probably deny its existence.

The destructive criticism which I have been offering in a good part of this book has, however, been no more deliberately or solely destructive than is a mother's insistence upon her growing boy relinquishing, say, the habit of sucking his thumb—a habit not only pleasurable but in an earlier stage natural and reasonable enough—no more so than the efforts of a teacher to rid his pupils, when they are of an age to profit by the strong meat of thought, from the inevitably naïve views of childhood and of uninstructed everyday, to the truer and more satisfying conclusions of organized science and philosophy. Let me illuminate my meaning from biology—and this not merely because it happens to be my own science, but because the whole problem with which this book attempts to deal, the problem of religion, is itself in one quite real sense a biological problem.

If some discarnate spirit, not knowing what the future was to bring forth, had been able to visit this globe and to see its conditions say every forty million years, what would have been his report? Assuredly it would always have been good. At the beginning the existence of life where before there had been no life would have been a notable fact. Later the vision of elaborated life, the hosts of strange and beautiful marine creatures, heavy-armoured or pellucid-swimming, brilliant coral and flower-like seaanemone, would again have been good. It would have seemed good when the first fish, dominating the rest of life through power of brain and backbone, sailed the seas; when plants first learnt to colonize the land, hitherto barren; when the first trees towered to new heights, and the first insects practised life's new power of flight among them. If the imaginary observer had seen the world in the middle of the Secondary epoch, he could not fail to have been struck by the amazing creatures he saw. The insects had been first on land; but new forms of life now dominated the scene. The reptiles, outdistancing the amphibia from which they had sprung, luxuriated in every form. There were reptilian creatures unrivalled for sheer bulk; others as rapid as racehorses; others which beat the fishes at their own game and had become kings of the sea; still others that were veritable dragons of the air, far outdistancing insects in speed and size alike. There would have been things that did not seem so good, it is true. As the winter came round, the activity of these embodiments of the vital spirit would have flagged, and whole realms of the earth's surface must have been permanently closed to their cold blood; the law of life was rapine and death; brute force and bulk were as successful as accuracy of perception or speed. None the less it would have seemed natural and right to accept all these evils as the price of the good.

But if he had again visited the earth in the later middle of the next, or Tertiary, epoch, he would have found a very different picture. The reptiles, though surviving in various forms, were then no longer dominant, and all their most remarkable types had perished off the face of the earth. The picture of life would have been very much like that which the traveller views to-day in the unspoilt parts of East Africa and Uganda; and all who have seen that life testify to the thrill of its variety and vigorous beauty. Some of the apparently inevitable drawbacks of Secondary life have been overcome. Life, in the form of birds and mammals, is no longer subject to the arbitrary changes in its proper activity inflicted by the changing temperature of the outer world : it has surmounted the difficulty by maintaining its own inner environment at a constant temperature. By this device it has been able to colonize parts of the world untenanted before : even the Arctic is invaded by this new warm-blooded life. What is more, bulk and armour, which seemed so necessary and indeed so magnificent in the old reptiles, have largely been discarded; and in their place are the better and more beautiful devices of speed, alertness, and intelligence. The old struggle still remains, however, and progress is still achieved mainly through the ruthlessness of selective death.

This mechanism, he would find, had always been the most powerful agency for change in evolution, and he might well be pardoned if he supposed that it was the sole possible agency. Knowledge, too, for all the improvement of the ages, was still limited in its quality, and still died with its possessor. Would it have seemed probable or even possible that this barrier could be overcome? And yet, had our imaginary visitor come once again when man was in possession of the earth, he would have had to revise all his ideas of the possible, and to admit that the good which he had recognized in earlier life, though certainly still good, was extremely imperfect. Indeed, many of the qualities which, when the old scheme of life is considered by itself, can properly be called good, seem of a dubious goodness or wholly evil when considered in relation to the new state of affairs. How is it possible to consider natural selection an ideal method, in spite of its successes, if new methods of conscious planning, less wasteful, less lengthy, and apparently more successful, are now available?

Again, the possibility of accumulating knowledge over generations makes all the short-range knowledge of all other organisms seem almost pitiful; and even within human history, the organization of tested knowledge according to the scientific method not only makes the earlier hit-or-miss procedures look foolish, but makes it actually wrong to utilize them when this something better is available.

There is no reason for supposing that any particular stage of life is the last word in evolution. Just as good a claim to be the " crown of creation " could have been made for the great age of Reptiles, or for the late Tertiary, as for our present phase of human life. Man is an organism, and not only may his knowledge and his power increase out of all dreaming, but his very nature may as well be changed as that of the reptile which was transformed to mammal or the monkey-being who grew through ape to man.

What is the moral? Simply this : that thought evolves equally with life : that religious systems which were inevitable products of humanity's childhood or of its adolescent thinking, which may indeed have been the necessary scaffolding for some better building, are not for that reason final : that ideas which in their time and season meant immense advance, concepts which were not only solidly good but as good as it was possible for man to make them in the circumstances, may actually become harmful when circumstances alter and the old ideas are found to be hindering the progress of new and better ideas. Exactly the same state of affairs may be found in the field of industry and invention.

But on the other hand, in spite of vested interests, conservatism, and prejudice, the progress of economic invention is to-day at least a fairly rapid one. Compared with progress in established religious systems of thought it is extremely speedy. What is the reason for this difference? The answer, I think, is twofold. In the first place, and most important, stands the fact of the sacredness of religious beliefs.

In the second place comes the belief that religious beliefs are different from other views, in that they have some supernatural sanction—that they are authoritative, or complete, or final, or are the product of a direct revelation from a personal God or one of his prophets. When all the world was superstitious and almost all men ignorant, when the authority of force was more necessary and the rate of change much slower, then such notions (for whatever reasons they were held) may have been of valuable service in helping to spread and to lend force to the purer and nobler ideas attained by the few rare spirits who thought for themselves. But to-day, when all knowledge is at the door of any one who can read, to be had almost for the asking, when humanity can look round and see the present accurately in its relation with nature and with man's past development—to-day any such view is definitely pernicious.

Beliefs, we cannot too often remind ourselves, are only tools of the human mind. They may be the useful but lightly regarded things we know as hypotheses, useful to busy science as a screw-driver or a pair of pliers is useful round the house; or the larger, more firmly grounded erections known as scientific theories, built up so strongly and with so much of supporting fact that a great deal is rightly demanded of any rival claim before the old theory is discarded; or violently-held but slenderly-grounded beliefs, like some of those which any student of comparative religion will have come across, or like those which sweep across a country in time of war, which are of grave and often terrible importance in their effects, although they crumble to pieces once the cool light of day is let in upon them; or the beliefs of everyday, often but half-conscious, compounded of intuition and prejudice, emotion and shrewdness, which guide most actions of most men and women in the routine of business and social intercourse.

If I have attacked certain aspects of certain religious systems it is not because I have any wish to attack the religious impulse; nor do I think that their destruction would leave an unfilled gap. If the whole great edifice of mediævalist theology were to crumble away to nothing, the religious feeling native to humanity would speedily enough build up something else which could be put in its place.

But what, I shall be asked, is there which can be put in its place? Is it not presumption even to think that there is something which can fitly be put in its place?

If, however, as I believe, all theologies and all religious experiences are, as a matter of fact, entirely products of the human spirit, is it not much greater presumption to invoke the Divine in support of a particular belief, to assert that religious belief stands on a different footing from other beliefs, and to exploit God for the purposes of theological controversy?

The view that I would like to put forward is presumptuous, yes—but also humble. No religious outlook which takes account of nature and man as they really are but must mingle the contrasted elements of pride and humility—humility, in the sense of littleness when we confront our small and transitory selves with the majesty and permanence of life and the universe; pride, when we take heart and remember of what achievements man is capable—" what a piece of work is a man!"—and that each of our individual lives is unique, in a real sense ultimate, and reaches out to touch infinite heights and depths.

No one who will turn his eyes upon himself and his own being and contemplate the spectacle in a spirit of detachment from practical details of everyday, so far as possible *sub specie æternitatis*, but will come to feel something of reverence at what we may call the miracle of the mere existence of such an organization of material and mental qualities. If he has had some scientific training, his sense of wonder will be increased. This *man* is a small block of the general substance of which the whole universe is formed, just as is a stone or a stream or a piece of bread; but it has come to possess, as the result of evolution, the most surprising qualities. This piece of world-stuff possesses not only form and movement, but the capacity for knowing about other parts of the world, even stars a thousand light-years off, events ten million years ago. It possesses the capacity for will, and with will and knowledge working together has learnt to control in notable degree both outer nature and its own nature. In some ways most extraordinary of all, it possesses the capacity for feeling, and for feeling in such a way that before some emotions all practical considerations fall away as unimportant; through feeling, this sentient portion of the world-continuum may be exalted to states which have value higher than anything else in the same world-continuum, and are often regarded as having absolute value.

Here is a mass of a few kilograms, of substance that is indivisibly one (both its matter and spirit), by nature and by origin, with the rest of the universe, which can weigh the sun and measure light's speed, which can harness the tides and organize the electric forces of matter to its profit, which is not content with huts or shelters, but must build Chartres or the Parthenon; which can transform sexual desire into

the love of a Dante for his Beatrice; which can not
only be raised to ineffable heights at the sight of
natural beauty or find "thoughts too deep for
tears" in a common flower, but can create new
countries and even heavens of its own, through
music, poetry, and art, to which it may be translated,
albeit temporarily, from this practical world; which
is never content with the actual, and lives not by
bread alone; which is always not only surmounting
what it thought were the limitations of its nature,
but, in individual and social development alike,
transcending its own nature and emerging in new-
ness of achievement.

    •   •   •   •   •

What is left now for me is to make my statement
of my own attitude. Others may agree or disagree.
Let them at least remember that agreement or disagreement with this attitude has little to do with
agreement or disagreement with this or that part of
the views which helped determine it, and with the
correctness or otherwise of the discussion that has
gone before. For an attitude of mind or a statement
of belief is a complex, organic thing, involving all
sorts of hidden springs of personality, all kinds of
thoughts never properly looked at in the light of
conscious day, involving also in its construction
something of creative activity, which itself (like the
creative activity of an artist) may be good or bad,
so that good materials may be spoilt by the use
which is made of them.

    •   •   •   •

I believe first and foremost that life is not merely
worth living, but intensely precious: and that the
supreme object of life is to live; or, if you like to
turn it round, that the great object of living is to
attain more life—more in quality as well as quantity.
We men are from one point of view mere trivial mi-
crobes, but from another the crown of creation: and
both views are true, and we must hold them together,

interpenetrating, in our thought. From the point of view of the stellar universe, whose size and meaningless spaces baffle comprehension and belief, man may be a mere nothing, and all his efforts destined to disappear like the web of a spider brushed down from the corner of a little room in the basement of a palace; but meanwhile he is engaged upon a task which is the most valuable of any known, the most valuable which by him can be imagined, the task of imposing mind and spirit upon matter and outer force. This he does by confronting the chaos of outer happenings with his intellect, and generating ordered knowledge; with his æsthetic sense, and generating beauty; with his purpose, and generating control of nature; with his ethical sense and his sense of humour, and generating character; with his reverence, and generating religion. In a phrase, he is a living mill or vital machine into which the world of brute reality is poured in all its rawness, to emerge, a new reality on a higher level, as a world of values.

For man to live fully it is necessary for him, as for every other organism, to be adapted to his surroundings; but man can do so on a new level, denied to other organisms, in the world of mind. His life, if it is to be the best life possible, must be seen, felt, and practically lived in its relation to the rest of the universe. If he fails to take account of any essential of reality, or if he misinterprets it, woe to him : the omission or the mistake will bring its retribution.

To this task of relating his life to the rest of reality he must bring all his powers; but the mortar which must hold all together if the construction is to hold is the spirit of love and reverence. Such a construction so held together is a true and developed religion.

That is what orthodox theism means when it says that the knowledge and love of God is the first duty of man. But orthodox religions have kept primitive ideas of supernaturalism and of personality in God which render their view more difficult, less simple,

H

more ambitious, less real. Those ideas are idols, and need to be destroyed like other idols.

I believe that we must learn all we can of nature. A knowledge of matter and energy in lifeless and living systems is the first requisite, for we must know the world in which we live if we wish to be adapted to it and, still more, if we wish to control it.

It is of equal importance for us to think out our scheme of values. What goals are ultimate, what desires are highest? Almost all philosophies and developed religions are agreed that truth, beauty, and goodness are the three human ultimates, to be desired for their own sakes, to be desired above all else. At least, they are agreed in theory; in practice, difficulties crop up as to interpretation and practical methods. But it is worth while affirming fundamental theories, however many practical difficulties occur in their application.

Some would say that sanctity is another ultimate. I believe rather that reverence, or the capacity for discovering the sanctity of things, is a way of approach which is necessary if we are to advance beyond a certain point in the quest for the three highest values. Reverence then would be in the same category as love, joy, patience, disinterested curiosity, tolerance, and humour, as being a necessary way in which the mind shall walk if it is to achieve the things worth achieving.

I believe that life, with human nature in its forefront, is the means of giving actuality to the ideal; that in this consists our true destiny; that the secret of making progress in this task is to train the spirit to all disinterested activity—disinterested love of what is brave and happy, of beauty, of knowledge, of ministering to those that suffer, those that are in ignorance or in that other, moral darkness; that this disinterested love, once truly gained, will bring with it all the other ways of advance, such as tolerance and humility, humour and reverence; that the highest expressions of human nature's faculty of bringing the ideal to dwell in actuality among men are works of art, including works of literature and architecture, are philosophies, laws of nature, and systems of scientific thought, are the characters of men and women, are ordered civilizations, are developed religions.

I believe also that the three regions of reality which I have mentioned, however diverse they be, however contradictory their main tendencies may seem, are all part of a single real unity. Dead matter has given birth to life : life has given birth to sensitive, purposeful, and intelligent mind; and mind not only desires to control matter, but is capable of the task.

.   .   .   .   .

I believe that it is both a foolish and a wicked phantasy of timorous thought to deny the reality of evil and of pain and suffering. They are intensely and terribly real. It is a false optimism to say that evil can always be overcome; but it can often be overcome. The overcoming of evil by good is not merely one of man's main goals; on the slow average it is being accomplished. The mystery of evil, however, is not only its existence; it lies also in the fact that out of evil may come good. Those are irreducible facts which we must simply accept. But they are also facts which are inevitable in a world which works like ours. If evolution is a devil-take-the-hindmost, in which mutual aid, kindness, and forethought are but late and sporadic comers upon the scene, its struggle for existence must give us the evil of tapeworms and plague and mosquitoes as well as the good of biological progress. If man as an imperfect organism on to whose animal nature new capacities are grafted, but are often given in strange combination by the hand of heredity, often thwarted and distorted by environment, then we shall expect cruelties and hurts, perversions and fears, hatreds and selfishness, and all their evil effects. We shall expect them, but we shall try to overcome them. We shall expect them, and accept them as a challenge; but need not continue to torment our souls with the question of why an imaginary creator, to whom we have ascribed our own ideals of foresight and benevolence, should have inserted evil into the scheme of things.

Pain, in spite of all that has been written about the difficulty of comprehending the reason for its existence, is simpler. It is a biological necessity. Without physical pain there could be no adapted life, no progressive evolution. Without mental suffering there could be no mental progress. Pain, once in existence, may inflict itself in biologically useless ways as well as useful ones, just as may intellectual or æsthetic pleasure. It may inflict itself in spiritually useless ones too; for though pain and suffering may be necessary ingredients of many a great character, they may be sterile. Sterile pain is a challenge like evil; it is for us to do our best to make it impossible. Indeed, our aim must be constantly the reduction of all pain; for though it can often be turned to good, without that effort and expense of soul the good might have been greater. At all events we shall certainly never abolish it, and need be deterred by no moral or theological scruples, such as made themselves heard when chloroform was first used in childbirth, in our attempts to be rid of it. What must be remembered, however, is the fact that pain is an instrument of adaptation, and that lesser pain in the present may ensure better adaptation and so forestall much greater pain in the future.

I believe that sin exists, and the sense of sin. But I believe that the exaggeration of the sense of sin, the over-stressing of the idea that it is a necessary preliminary to salvation (which is found in a number of Christian sects) is pernicious.

While it is true that we all fall far short, not merely of perfection but of our reasonable possibilities, and that it is profitable for our mental health to turn our thoughts regularly inwards upon our short-comings, yet constant over-emphasis on sin leads not only to frequent hypocrisy, but to a wrong habit of mind and a failure to realize as much of positive good as would otherwise be the case.

Once it is recognized that the sense of sin is often, and especially in adolescence, a mental disease, something to be avoided if possible and got over (like the measles) with the utmost celerity, instead of being paraded as admirable, the great step will have been taken. It is nothing to be ashamed of, any more than measles; but, also like the measles, it is nothing to be proud of. I believe that the religion of the future will have as one of its great aims the saving of man from an exaggerated sense of sin by prevention of childish conflicts. Just as preventive medicine and public health are becoming more and more important and will make the cure of the individual less and less necessary, so I believe that what by analogy may be called " preventive religion " and general spiritual hygiene will become more important, and will make some of the methods of present-day Christianity look as crude and barbaric as does bleeding or the universal black draught to modern scientific medicine.

I believe in grace and the sense of grace. I do not believe in it as a gift from divine power, but in the fact of its existence as a special inner illumination and peace which comes when conflicts are resolved on a high plane, when æsthetic or intellectual insight is vouchsafed, whenever, in fact, an unexpected or perhaps undeserved moment of spiritual achievement is thrust on the mind, and the mental state is coloured (sometimes half-consciously) with the feeling best described as sacramental. I believe that religion has arrogated to itself, quite unjustly, the exclusive possession of this "grace"; but that in reality it operates in every sphere of the mind's life.

I believe that its connection with the sense of sin has been much over-emphasized; and that indeed the more a human being is without a sense of sin, the more harmonious and unthwarted his development, the more numerous and the more glorious may be expected to be the graces and illuminations which sanctify and give value to his life.

I believe that the individual attains his supreme satisfactions in precisely these moments. They are the moments in which he with his mortal fingers touches the absolute. There is an absolute of truth; and though no one can grasp all truth or, what comes to the same thing, all the implications of a single truth, yet we may solve the particular problem we have held before us, we may see in a flash our solution, its truth, and its relation to many of our other ideas. That is Promethean: that is the bringing of the fire of absolute truth from its unrealized state to make it dwell in this phenomenal world.

In just the same way we can touch the absolute of beauty and, through our spirit, perceive it investing common things and common vision; we can touch the absolute of goodness and realize something of the good in a single course of action. There is an absolute of harmony and unity; we can experience in ourselves a moment of that harmony when we succeed in adjusting the diverse and conflicting elements of our life, as they happen to exist at the time, all in a single unity. It is but momentary; we must continue to grow, and new equilibria will come to be necessary; but in that moment we shall have tasted a knowledge which is absolute, and embodied something of ideal harmony in our actual temporal being. There is an absolute of righteousness; that, too, we can touch by moments; and this grace is most intensely felt when it rescues us from the opposite extreme, of a sense of sin or unrighteousness.

But it is simply not a fact that it is the exclusive privilege of Christian believers. There is a grace of holiness which can be attained in love; without it ungratified desire is pain, desire gratified is merely transitory release from tension, or satiety and revulsion—but, with it superadded, ungratified desire is itself desirable, prayer and beauty are one, gratified desire a sacramental transcendence of the boundaries of the self, on which, as Blake says, " the soul expands her wing."

In all these and many other ways we may touch the absolute, sacramentally transcend ourselves. It is in this sphere that virtue is its own reward; this is the true coin in which human nature receives its best gifts, most valued because not deserved or simply earned as a right, but (I repeat) a present, a gift distilling out of the inner nature of things.

On the other hand the spirit must labour for wages too, and earn them. I believe that to live solely or mainly for these moments of transcendence, whether in religion, or love, or beauty of art or nature, or intellect, is mere selfishness. Like other selfishness, it brings its own penalties, which may be no less severe in spite of their existence not being consciously realized. The world demands work. Work is needed for the mere maintenance of life; more work is needed for the maintenance of a particular level of civilization; still more work is needed if we look to the future and aim at giving later generations better chances of fuller life.

I believe that religion is peculiarly liable to abuse. This is so because it should and can involve the patient approach of the self to as much of reality as it can grasp, and yet at the same time it is an answer to an imperious demand for certitude, for a basis on which, here and at once, to build our few short years of living. What wonder, then, if a hasty answer is often preferred to long search, or pretended certitude to reverent doubt? What wonder that the cramped human being compensates itself for the injustices of this world by indulging in phantasies concerning the next, or that the limitation of outlook which is the lot of so many is reflected in a one-sided creed? Finally, it concerns itself, and must concern itself, largely with beliefs. The psychological mechanism of belief being what it is, small wonder that beliefs, however incredible or contradictory, are not merely held, but held with tenacity and violence.

Just because religion can concern the whole personality on the one hand, and the rest of the universe on the other, just because it can help to make unity and order out of diversity and chaos, just because it aspires to so much, just because of all this can it so easily fall short and go astray.

The religious attitude of mind, which demands a reverent approach to reality, is necessary if the best use is to be made of human life, and if the varied activities and achievements of man are to be properly organized into a coherent whole; but it is by no means always necessary or even desirable as a component of any given activity or as a means towards any given achievement.

To be always religious is as intolerable as to be always laughing, or always working, or always playing golf. For a man to have a religious disposition it is no more necessary for religious feeling to be always in possession of the mind than it is for a man of a humorous disposition to be incapable of sentiment or seriousness. The mere variety of human nature and human activity is its richness and its charm; and to give each faculty and each approach to reality its turn and its due place in life is to live not only fully but truly.

This brings me to tolerance. I believe in tolerance because variety is spiritual richness, and because variety and indeed opposition is necessary for the highest achievements of individuals and of civilizations.

If our religion is a true religion, a religion of fuller life, it must both tolerate and reverence variety. But our tolerance must not be merely passive, a tired intellectual gesture; it must be active, springing from the belief and knowledge that truth is too large to be revealed in but one form, or one creed, or one way of life. We must accept the hard saying that out of diversity alone comes advance, and that any one human mind is too small to grasp more than a little truth, to live more than a little reality.

I believe that one of the greatest defects of our modern world is its lack of a religion of its own, and the accompanying disruption of its thought and aims. Since the Middle Ages, life's centre of gravity has shifted from heaven to earth. For a hypothetical future existence called in to redress the balance of this, man has taken in exchange the certainty of present reality, with all its imperfections, but with all its perfectibility. Science has been the chief instrument of the new vision, organization and foresight its watchwords, harnessed power, whether of natural forces or of wealth, its instrument. But religion, speaking broadly, has remained through all these centuries adapted to the old state of things, not to the new.

The situation to-day is deplorable. The great bulk of the religious spirit, with all its potentialities for promoting human unity, for providing busy man with peace and refreshment, for helping humanity in its task of controlling evolution (which is only a more accurate way of saying the bringing to pass of the kingdom of God upon earth), for stressing the permanent satisfactions and highest values in the welter of daily existence, is locked up in a theological strong-box, hidden away from half humanity in a fairy-story land.

The bulk of creative human endeavour, on the other hand, either pays only lip-service to organized religion, or is in opposition. It does not and will not inhabit that mythological land; it has different values, different standards, different aims. It is science, art, industry, commerce, government: it is of this world. Its best science is bound up with this life. Its best glories are in the here and now—illuminations, ecstasies, glories of love, joy, peace; its furthest aims are in this world's future, its greatest task is to work so that truth and goodness, beauty and holiness may increasingly be incarnated. By existing religions it is offered personal salvation at the price of surrendering this world or subordinating it to the next. But it knows that the task of its soul is to animate this world. And what shall it profit a man if he gain the whole next world and lose his own soul? For he who would save his soul shall surely lose it.

I believe that the great sacrifice needed for religion is that of her old certitude, to be offered up on the altar of humility. And that demanded by organized science, and all the doers of good works and planners of the future to boot, is that of all narrowness and aggressiveness, to be offered on the altar of reverence and imaginative love. But to-day the sacrifice of organized religion is more necessary and more called for than that of science, and failure to make it will be not only more blameworthy but, from her own standpoint, more foolish.

If that sacrifice is not made there will be strife. Great is truth, and shall prevail: but the day of her prevailing will then be long delayed, and the endeavourers of this world will be forced to dig their own wells to the waters which she inhabits, with expense of labour and time and spirit, when this sacrifice on the part of organized religion would have at once made them accessible to all.

I have no doubt of the ultimate issue. The verdict of the trend of human history, in the fifteen thousand years since civilization dawned in the later Old Stone Age, is too clear to permit a doubt. But in what way it will come, and after how long, and what it will be like, the future religion of this world and of all humanity—that nobody can know.

One can only guess : that it will take a long time; that it will not be the work of any single founder, but will be achieved through the gradual permeation of society by knowledge and disciplined thought as education spreads and becomes more effective; that religion by abandoning some of its pretensions will become accessible to more people, and more vital in the life of the community; and that the two necessities of scientific means and ideal ends will become more fruitfully linked as the one increasing purpose is more clearly seen. Hard fact and transforming value together build future reality. I believe that the whole duty of man can be summed up in the words : more life, for your neighbour as for yourself. And I believe that man, though not without perplexity, effort, and pain, can fulfil this duty and gradually achieve his destiny.

A religion which takes this as its central core and interprets it with wide vision, both of the possibilities open to man and of the limitations in which he is confined, will be a true religion, because it is coterminous with life; it will encourage the growth of life, and will itself grow with that growth.

I believe in the religion of life.

INDEX